THEY ROSE AGAIN

THEY ROSE AGAIN

Edited by Harry Conroy

Words by Gregor Kyle, Donna Nicholson and Brian McGeachan

Photographs by Paul McSherry

LINDSAY
PUBLICATIONS

First Published in 2003 by Lindsay Publications, Glasgow

Copyright © *Scottish Catholic Observer*
History of Catholic Church © Brian McGeachan
Individual chapters as acknowledged © Gregor Kyle
and © Donna Nicholson
Photographs © Paul McSherry

ISBN 1 898169 29 2

A CIP record of this publication is available from the British publisher

Designed and typeset by Eric Mitchell, Glasgow and C & R Graphics, Cumbernauld

Printed and bound by Oriental Press, U.A.E.

ACKNOWLEDGEMENTS

I WISH TO ACKNOWLEDGE the enthusiasm in putting together this book which first appeared as a series of articles in the *Scottish Catholic Observer*. Entitled Faith of Our Fathers, they were written by Gregor Kyle and Donna Nicholson, both staff reporters and freelance writer Brian McGeachan, who compiled the history of the Catholic Church 1560–1829 material attached to each chapter.

Thanks also to Paul McSherry, our freelance photographer, who travelled throughout Scotland capturing many historic Church sites used in this book.

To Ignatius Kusiak, managing director of the *Catholic Herald Ltd,* owner of the *Scottish Catholic Observer,* my grateful thanks for his willingness to back the publication and also to Donald MacDonald, proprietor of Lindsay publications, who embraced the valuable contribution this book will make to raising awareness of our history.

I also appreciate the advice given by the newly-installed Archbishop Mario Conti of Glasgow for his interpretation of events and confirmation of dates in some of the chapters. The Archbishop's support of our Scottish Heritage is well known and his knowledge was of immense help.

I would also thank our Publishing consultant, Eric Mitchell, who always had an eye on deadlines and for the fine detail of the book ensuring that we finished with a book which does justice to the subject. To the staff of C & R Graphics for maintaining a high-quality publication.

Finally I express the hope that this book will be read and enjoyed by those communities it features within its covers.

HARRY CONROY,
November 2002

DEDICATION

This book is dedicated to all who have held on to their faith,
no matter what faith, during troubled times

CONTENTS

Chapters 1. 14, 15 by Donna Nicholson and Brian McGeachan

Chapters 2–13 by Gregor Kyle and Brian McGeachan

PREFACE

I AM HAPPY TO APPLAUD the enterprise and energy of the authors of this book, it is intended by them to provide a concise narrative of some of the most significant sites of the Catholic Church in post-reformation Scotland.

The stories told within these chapters is one of persecution and of valour, of loss and gain. It should provide an inspiration to us all.

My hope is that this book will be widely read and perhaps stimulate renewed interest in the history of the Church in our land.

+Mario Conti
Archbishop of Glasgow

ST NINIAN

THE RELICS OF ST NINIAN at Whithorn have attracted pilgrims from across the world for centuries. The focus of pilgrimage has shifted in modern times from Whithorn to the cave on the coast used by Ninian. Arriving by sea pilgrims landed at the Isle of Whithorn just a few miles south of Whithorn. Today the ruins of a fourteenth-century church to St Ninian look out over the sea above the original landing place.

When Ninian established a settlement at Whithorn in 397 it was probably the first Christian place of worship north of Hadrian's Wall and consisted of a white church and a few small houses with central hearths. The settlement was abandoned 150 years later. Two shrines were erected at the site. Years later additional shrines were added, along with a graveyard. Historians believe one of the shrines must have been particularly important as its four internal pillars formed the central focus of the next church to be built there in the seventh century. This shrine was incorporated into a more substantial church built after the Northumbrians established a bishopric at Whithorn in 730.

In 1307 Whithorn became an ecclesiastical burgh and the Cathedral increased in size and importance until the Reformation in 1560 when pilgrimage was banned in Scotland. Whithorn lost its status and, like the many abbeys around Wigtownshire, was left empty and became derelict.

Now at the site is the priory museum run by Historic Scotland which boasts 'the largest and most important collection of Early Christian and Dark Age carved stones in south-west Scotland'. They include stones from St Ninian's Cave as well as the Latinus Stone, the oldest Christian monument in Scotland, carved around 450.

Nothing of the first buildings has survived but the ruins of the priory and Cathedral built in the twelfth century can still be seen. The ruined nave shows that although pilgrimage was banned during the Reformation in Scotland and the whole Cathedral complex at Whithorn fell into ruin, work continued on the nave before it was finally abandoned in 1822. What is left of the south wall shows the development of the building from the twelfth to eighteenth centuries and indicates the splendour of the original complex in the days when it was 'the resort of Kings'.

The Arch of the Gatehouse, by which pilgrims passed into the monastic precinct, has also survived from the Middle Ages.

The old church and graveyard at Whithorn stand on the site of Ninian's priory

The altar at the rear of the modern day St Martin and St Ninian's Church

Galloway's Christian tradition dates back to the early fifth century when the Britons established themselves into small communities. They followed the practices of the Roman Church which had flourished throughout the Roman provinces of Britannia a century earlier. Two surviving mid-fifth-century gravestones show evidence of these early communities living in Whithorn and Kirkmadrine.

The early seeds of Christianity were brought to this area by the man we have come to know as St Ninian. History is vague about him, even his name is a source of dispute with alternatives including Nynia, Ringan, Trinian, and Finian. Excavations at Whithorn have not uncovered his remains or any evidence of his church where he is thought to have been buried. So what do we really know about Ninian?

When he established himself in Galloway he built a church to St Martin of Tours, the Candida Casa, in the place now known as Whithorn. The Candida Casa was unique. Made of brick and not the usual timber, it was a famous landmark and is believed to have been built on the site which now holds the remains of the later Cathedral and Priory. From Ninian's original the town got its name, the White House, from the Old English words *hwit erne*.

Ninian is also recorded both by Aelred and the Venerable Bede, who mention the Candida Casa and he is credited with converting the Picts of Fife and Tayside to Christianity.

Janet Butterworth of the Whithorn Trust admitted:

> 'There's not a lot of evidence for Ninian. We know that during the Northumbrian period – about 700 – the cult of Ninian was established and it was seen as a place of sanctity. People visited the shrine because the Northumbrian church has what we think are guest quarters and feasts also took place there.'

The boom period in Galloway's economic history occurred between 1750 and 1850. This saw a rise in the population of the area, especially in Newton Stewart where it rose from 200 to more than 2000 in less than fifty years. Many of the people drawn to the area by the prospect of employment were Catholics from Ireland. The congregation at Our Lady and St Ninian's in Newton Stewart reached 3000. During this time the Catholic parishes in Wigtownshire were established.

In 1924 the first official Whithorn pilgrimage of the modern era took place but a work of literature written by a Benedictine monk mentions the festival of St Ninian in 1886. Despite the reinstatement of the pilgrimage in Whithorn, Catholics had to use a rented hall for Mass until the church of St Martin and St Ninian was built in 1960.

Today Wigtownshire is still a rural area and is a place of beauty and tranquillity with picturesque country villages and farmsteads. The parishes – St Joseph's in Stranraer, Our Lady and St Ninian in Newton Stewart, the Sacred Heart in Wigtown and St Martin and St Ninian in Whithorn – now serve smaller parishes than the originals.

THE ANCIENT LAND

Wigtownshire in the south-west of Scotland is where the seeds of Christian heritage were first sown. Around the countryside are ruins testifying to the changing nature of religious culture throughout the past 1500 years.

The Royal Burgh of Whithorn claims a special place in history as the home of St Ninian, the first man to bring the teachings of Christ to Scotland. Once a thriving centre of both trade and pilgrimage rivalling both the Holy Land and Europe it is now a quiet county town. Pilgrims, including royalty, came from all over to visit the

The fourteenth century church to St Ninian at the Isle of Whithorn

Interior of ruined church on the Isle of Whithorn

shrine of St Ninian and as the cult grew so did the development of Wigtownshire.

Due to the work of archaeologists and historians we know more about Ninian. It is not surprising he chose Whithorn as the site for his mission. Its position, three miles inland from the southern tip of the region, makes it ideally accessible for pilgrims arriving by sea.

Janet Butterworth of the Whithorn Trust explained:

'In those days the quickest, easiest and safest way to travel was by sea. Whithorn was ideal for anyone coming from England, the Isle of Man, Ireland, the north and right up from the Mediterranean.

The evidence we've uncovered shows we've got trade with the Mediterranean going on early because of the position and although we've got Roman influences there's no evidence of Romans in situ. Since work began datable evidence from 415 has been uncovered and the results show it was a very active area.

Smelting was being done and there was a considerable amount of advanced technology. Normally a Roman settlement brings in technology but something else is a driving force – the Church is organising the people.'

Around 700, about 300 years after Ninian is said to have died, there is evidence that the cult of Ninian had been well established.

'From 850 there is evidence of lots of small houses with fires in the corners, games were played, weaving and spinning were done and trade increased. It is believed that cats may have been farmed for their pelts and a factory system set up working with antlers and making objects, for example, combs.

These people were not marauding Vikings but were settled and trading. The Church was enlarging and therefore the people were practising their Christian beliefs. Evidence of pilgrims coming to Whithorn has been found on the roadway leading to the Cathedral.'

By the twelfth century Whithorn, taking its name from the Old English words for white house, *hwit erne*, in reference to Candida Casa church – housed the Cathedral of Galloway, with the relics of St Ninian enshrined in the church.

In the years that followed the Church continued to grow and prosper. The shrine was visited by Scotland's leaders, namely Robert the Bruce, King David II, King James IV and Mary, Queen of Scots. Disruption lay ahead with the onslaught of the Reformation in 1560.

THE CHURCH IN SCOTLAND

THE SEEDS OF DESTRUCTION were sown long before the Reformation. As the established Church, politics and the secular rights of kings occupied much of its attention in the thirteenth century. It was a willing participant and an authority used by competing claims for kingship.

Since the Middle Ages the Catholic Church in Scotland had been the pre-eminent power and in April 1286 the Scottish Parliament nominated six administrators to act as guardians of the realm. They included Bishop Fraser of St Andrews and Bishop Wishart of Glasgow. It was a reflection of the close relationship that existed between the State and the Catholic Church.

At the time of the death of Alexander III his granddaughter Princess Margaret was in Norway. Her right to the crown had already been formally recognised but she died on the way to Scotland, causing rival power bases to be set up by Robert Bruce and John Baliol.

Edward I of England, a fierce opponent of Scottish independence, saw this precarious situation as an aid in uniting his Kingdom with Scotland. A bloody conflict ensued between the two nations until 1300, when Edward granted a truce to the Scots, principally through the intervention of Pope Boniface VIII. An emissary had been sent to Rome earlier seeking the Pope's support for Scotland. He wrote to Edward reminding him that the nation had been from the earliest times a fief of the Holy See, proving by various arguments that England had no right to the fealty of the Scottish Crown.

By mid-1302 the Pope appeared to have lost his enthusiasm for the Scottish cause and in August he wrote to the bishops of Scotland imploring them to stop their opposition to Edward.

Among the prelates who most openly supported the cause for Scottish independence was Robert Wishart, the Bishop of Glasgow. Having previously absolved Robert Bruce from murder, he crowned him at Scone in 1306.

After the Battle of Methven in 1306, Bishop Lamberton of St Andrews and the Abbot of Scone were taken prisoner by the Earl of Pembroke and sent to England in chains. The Church's profile as a powerful force would continue but at a cost.

In the 1890 *History of the Catholic Church*, Canon Alphons Bellesheim wrote:

> '*The field of ecclesiastical history during the reign of Robert III in the early fifteenth century is singularly barren of important events.*
>
> *The period was one in which the State appeared to have shaken off to some extent the salutary influence of the Church and the close connection which had existed between them during the Middle Ages was considerably loosened.*
>
> *The exile of the Popes at Avignon had just come to an end and the painful spectacle of a disputed Papal election was again, after many centuries, presented to Christendom.*
>
> *The result of this state of things was manifested in a visible weakening of respect for spiritual power; and in Scotland, as elsewhere, we find traces of the antagonism between the Church and State, which was afterwards to assume such fatal proportions.*'

OLD AUCHENTROIG

THE SCOTTISH BASE of the St Patrick's Missionary Society lies hidden in the farming heartlands of Stirlingshire. More commonly known in Scotland as the Kiltegan Fathers, the priests have been based in the area since 1965. Situated a few miles outside the village of Buchlyvie their home is a grand memorial to a time in Scotland's history which still fires the imagination.

To reach the house you make a turn off a country road, up a long path, flanked by evergreens and tall trees. At the end of the path you look across the heart of the glen at a view dominated by the Victorian mansion, home to the priests.

Behind this mansion lies a small white house, which has survived acts of banditry and siege and to this day bears the marks made by a Scottish folk hero. Known as Old Auchentroig, the house, built in 1702, was home to one of the oldest families in Stirlingshire, the MacLachlans of Auchentroig. Eight years later an incident took place during the fair in nearby Aberfoyle, triggering a series of events which have immortalised the name of Old Auchentroig in local history.

The annual fair attracted families from throughout the Stirlingshire area. It was an opportunity to mix business with pleasure, trading goods and meeting old friends. However in the volatile years of the early eighteenth century the fair attracted more than its share of trouble. Stirlingshire was the haunt and unofficial kingdom of Rob Roy MacGregor. Even today his name is visible above local pubs, inns and businesses and almost any local on any road can point to some ancient tree or stump reputed to be the great man's hiding place. A fierce patriot and fiercer highwayman, MacGregor lived in his clan's former lands, which lay close to those of MacLachlan.

During the fair of 1710 one MacLachlan made the mistake of offending MacGregor – an act which was nothing short of suicidal. A peeved Rob Roy and his clansmen laid siege to Old Auchentroig. Although unsuccessful in his attempt to abduct the laird and his son, the outlaw did make off with all the MacLachlans' cattle and sheep. Despite the haul, Rob Roy still felt aggrieved and later returned to the house for another try. This time he decided

Old Auchentroig

The door that still bears the scars of the attack

Recently restored by the National Trust for Scotland, the house is recognised as a 'remarkably unaltered example of a typical Laird's House.' A local family rents the house from the Kiltegan Fathers and the original wooden door hangs on their kitchen wall, scorched but largely intact.

The Mansion House

The mansion built in the grounds of Old Auchentroig in 1850 has an equally interesting history.

Formerly the home of a Colonel Euing R Crawford the mansion and old house were sold in 1965 to the St Patrick's Missionaries. The mansion and surrounding grounds were to play a vital part in the future of the Church in Scotland. The house became a college for late vocations. Men entering the priesthood in their later years studied under the Kiltegan priests, the tranquil glen providing an

Inside the chapel

to smoke the laird out by setting fire to the bolted door and driving out the defenders. John MacLachlan and his son were taken hostage.

The laird and the outlaw struck up a friendship that was to signal the end of the enmity between the clans. The friendship did not extend to letting the laird off Scot free. Dumbarton Accounts hold records of a ransom of £100 being paid to Rob Roy in exchange for the men. The payment did include the return of the cattle stolen in the raid.

The incident led to a greater understanding between the Lowlanders and their Highland relatives. Tensions eased and the laird was often looked to as a trusted mediator during local disputes.

The MacLachlans remained in Old Auchentroig until 1884. Old Auchentroig survives and its front door still bears the scars of the McGregor assault.

The magnificent mansion house at Buchlyvie

the designs cut into the wood rather than carved from it.

Particularly eye-catching is a piece of what appears to be rock attached to the front of the altar.

'It's a fossil,' explained the Friar. 'There are four fish and you can make out the black spots of the eyes. People think that they are carved out but it was brought back from Brazil by one of the priests. Apparently there were a number lying around and the priests brought them home. One similar to this was sent to London for authentication and we are told that it could be one hundred or one hundred and twenty million years old – give or take twenty million. It's a nice feature on the altar.'

ideal backdrop for seminary life. The school eventually closed but the house remains a centre for the work of the Missionary Society. It also acts as a church to the local Catholic population in Buchlyvie. Its small chapel, initially used by students, now fills up every Sunday for Mass. Fr Reihill, who has been living in Buchlyvie since 1965, comments:

'The house is a promotions centre, we use it for our fundraising. Our magazine Africa is distributed from here and we also have charge of the parish. It recently became a parish since during the time of the college, local people attended the Sunday Mass and eventually we were asked to take on the parish. So now we are looking after churches in Balfron, Kippen and the chapel here in Buchlyvie.'

The small mansion chapel in Buchlyvie is original and beautiful, with many individual features from missions around the world.
The Stations of the Cross were made by an Irish craftsman with

The fossilised fish that came from Brazil

MURDER OF A CARDINAL

THE ASSASSINATION OF Cardinal David Beaton in 1546 heralded an era of bloodshed and acrimony, which continued to have repercussions for many years.

David Beaton was born in 1494, the third son of John Beaton of Balfour and Isabella Monypenny. The marriage of James, first Earl of Arran, to the daughter of Sir David Beaton of Creich made the future Cardinal a distant relative of the third earl, who afterwards became Regent of Scotland and heir-presumptive to the throne.

Beaton was educated at St Andrews until the age of 16 and in 1511 attended Glasgow University, while his uncle James Beaton was Archbishop of the city. He completed his education in Paris, gaining a knowledge of canon and civil law and in 1519, at the age of 25, he was appointed by James V as envoy at the Court of France.

The Archbishop bestowed upon his nephew the rectories of Campsie and Cambuslang and in 1523 obtained for his nephew a dispensation from wearing the monastic habit.

Returning to Scotland in 1525, David Beaton took his seat in Parliament as Abbot of Arbroath. One of the first acts of the young King James was to confer on David the post of Lord Privy Seal. This was the beginning of a close relationship between the two men. In 1533 David Beaton was sent to France as part of the sovereign's strategy of renewing the alliance with King Francis I and to negotiate a marriage between the king and a princess of the French royal house. After attending the wedding ceremony of King James and Princess Magdalen he returned with them to Scotland.

Following the early death of the young Queen within months of the marriage, the Lord Privy Seal was again in France requesting, on the King's behalf, the hand of Mary of Guise, widow of the Duke of Longueville.

In 1538 King James wrote to Pope Paul III requesting David Beaton be raised to the position of Cardinal. A month after he became Cardinal his uncle, the Archbishop of St Andrews, died and was succeeded by his nephew, who had six months previously been appointed coadjutor in that see. The strength of the new Cardinal's position and the close relationship he enjoyed with the King aroused the envy and distrust of King Henry VIII who viewed in his standing and policies the frustration of his own plans regarding Scotland.

Henry had, in 1539, sent Sir Ralph Sadler to James to determine the extent of the monarch's antipathy towards Reformed opinions and to undermine his confidence in the Cardinal. The ploy failed. But a grimmer fate awaited David Beaton.

Canon Alphons Bellesheim, in his four-volume (all periods), *History of The Catholic Church In Scotland*, comments:

> 'In May 1546 a pretext was found for the long-cherished plot. In a dispute which had arisen between the Cardinal and the young Master of Rothes, Norman Leslie, regarding the sale of an estate in Fife. He with his uncle, John Leslie, of Kirkaldy of Grange and James Melville, undertook to do the deed.
>
> 'On 28 May they arrived at St Andrews and at daybreak the following morning gained admission to the castle and killed the Cardinal with repeated blows of their swords
>
> 'John Knox is responsible for the statement that Melville added blasphemy to murder by avowing himself the messenger of God, who was sent to slay Beaton as an enemy of Christ and His holy Gospel.'

The assassination of Beaton signalled the start of a long and protracted battle between the established Church and the Protestant reformers.

ST JOSEPH'S AND ST PATRICK'S

THE INVERCLYDE AREA in the West of Scotland contains numerous examples of early religious sites, buried beneath centuries of progress. Inland from Inverkip, the remains of Chrisswell, one of the area's most historic Christian sites, lie encased beneath the concrete of the modern IBM information centre and the busy dual carriageway.

First known as Boag's well, it was a place of ancient pilgrimage with a sacred healing well. By the thirteenth century it had become known as Christ's Well, or Chrisswell, and it gave its name to the surrounding area. It served as the mission station for Inverclyde from 750 until around 1500. The well may have been discovered by the Celtic St Fillan, who, it is thought, travelled as a missionary throughout the region. He is widely credited with establishing Inverclyde's first Christian Mission near Largs, although the ancient St Fillan's Well and Chapel which stood there may have only been dedicated in his honour. The Manor Park Hotel now stands where the well and chapel were thought to have been. Chapelyard Farm and the ruined farm of Phillanswell hold the only clues as to the existence of this early place of worship.

By 1216 the village of Inverkip had been recognised by Rome as a parish and the centre of worship in Inverclyde. Its church, dedicated to the Holy Trinity, was said to be identical to the chapel at Chrisswell.

At that time Chrisswell was seen as an area of great spiritual importance. It was also the subject of many hearthside tales of witches, ghosts and the supernatural. Chrisswell was seen as a source of good while the nearby farm of 'Black' Dunrod was evil and said to house the devil incarnate.

By the 1980s, when IBM arrived and the Government sanctioned the building of new roads, all that remained of Chrisswell chapel and the nuns' house were two gable ends and piles of foundation stones. The plans for the road went right over consecrated ground and a local environmental group proposed that its history be preserved by making the ruin a feature on the central reservation. By that time, the land was being used as a campsite by travelling families and it was decided that the old ruin should be

St Joseph's and St Patrick's

The interior of St Joseph's and St Patrick's

removed altogether. As a result Chrisswell was buried beneath stone and concrete forever. Today all that remains of the ancient chapel and its lands is Chrisswell farm, which overlooks IBM.

However the story of the Church in this area is far from buried. By 1869 the growing Catholic community was gathering for worship in a small wooden hut in the village of Inverkip. The congregation included visiting Irish labourers who were working on the nearby railway line and the small church became known as 'The Holy Ground'. In 1887 the parish was transferred to Wemyss Bay where another wooden church was formally erected to serve the needs of the people. But the community was still growing and by the turn of the century a stone church, designed by the architect Pugin, was

St Joseph's and St Patrick's church

proposed for the village. The church of St Joseph's and St Patrick's was formally dedicated on 23 June 1901. The church was served by the priest based in Largs until the creation of the Paisley diocese in 1947–8.

In 1971, when Fr Vincent Grace arrived to serve the community, it was announced that St Joseph's and St Patrick's would be a parish in its own right.

In 2001 the church celebrated its centenary at a Mass celebrated by the parish priest Canon Joseph Quinn and Bishop John Mone.

The present church is a beautiful monument to this area's deep-rooted Catholic tradition and a constant reminder of the achievements of the past.

Prophet's curse

The fate of the demolished Catholic chapel at Chrisswell may have been sealed by a curse in the seventeenth century.

The area has long been a source of many dark legends, the most chilling of which is the story of Prophet Peden. The year 1638 saw the first disputes between the Episcopalian and Presbyterian Churches in Scotland after the proclaiming of the National Covenant. An influential Covenanter, the Prophet Peden was known to stay in the area, hiding from search parties in the hills around Spango Glen. One night, as storms battered the region, Peden was driven to seek refuge at the Chrisswell farmhouse. The occupants did not take too kindly to their unexpected visitor and as he was turned away Peden cried out that 'the traffic of the world would one day pass through their midst' and that 'the roof would be open to the winds of heaven.'

Today the IBM base that stands on the site transmits and conducts communications from around the world through the internet, while quite literally, 'the traffic of the world' races by on the dual carriageway in front.

Chrisswell's house and chapel were also laid bare to the elements, before the house was finally destroyed, as the rotting roof fell away.

The legends surrounding Chrisswell also involve national Scots history. As the story stands, the Stuart family were told that for as long as Chrisswell remained intact their rule would be guaranteed safe. When the house at Chrisswell fell into decline so did the fortunes of the Stuarts, who failed to recapture their former power in two Jacobite risings.

St Joseph's and St Patrick's church

THE SCOURGE OF THE CHURCH

THE FIGURE OF JOHN KNOX towers over the historical landscape of Scotland. To some the hero and to others the villain, he has become an almost mythical figure in the history of religious and political life. His controversial reputation makes it almost impossible to be impartial about him although a reappraisal of his influence is perhaps overdue.

John Knox was born in 1505 to middle-class parents at Gifford near Haddington. In 1531 he was sent to study at the University of Glasgow and earned approval in both philosophy and theology before being ordained a priest.

There is some doubt surrounding the date of Knox's adherence to the Reformed faith. Indeed very little is known of him before the murder of Cardinal Beaton.

It is said that he first openly declared himself a Protestant in 1542. That year Knox joined the conspirators in the castle of St Andrews who were plotting against the Regent, and were eventually overcome by forces who were drafted in from France. After his release from the French galleys in 1549, due to the intercession of Edward VI, John Knox was summoned to the Court and instructed to preach the Protestant doctrines.

He preached in the middle and south of England until 1553 when he took flight to Geneva. Here he formed an acquaintance with John Calvin. In 1559, when a conflict between the parties in Scotland seemed inevitable, John Knox returned to Scotland. It is then that forces conspired to bring about the Reformation.

This development propelled him into the forefront of the era of Protestant reformation in Scotland. The doctrines of predestination and the Elect, which were to be features of Scottish Presbyterianism, derive from St Augustine and are a recurring theme in the history of Christianity. The fervour with which they were incorporated into Scottish society owes more to the national character than to Knox himself.

In May of 1559 the self-appointed scourge of the Catholic Church in Scotland preached a provocative sermon in Perth. It undoubtedly established him as the intellectual leader of the Protestant movement, but objective forces were forging the final days of Catholic supremacy in the country.

There was the formation of the group of nobles who called themselves 'the lords of the Congregation'. Hostile to the French influence spawned by the regency of the Queen Mother, Mary of Guise, they looked to England for support.

Knox became Minister of St Giles in Edinburgh, which brought him into direct contact with the Queen, Mary Stuart. His opposition to Mary's stewardship is well-documented in his *History of the Reformation of Religion in the Realm of Scotland*.

St Mahew's altar

ST MAHEW'S CHURCH

IN THE DOORWAY of St Mahew's church in Cardross, near Dumbarton, stands a stone which is a lasting symbol of the bravery and faith of a Celtic saint whose actions saw the birth of a Christian tradition that survives to this day.

Tucked away on a back road behind the village of Cardross, the church of St Mahew stands on an ancient site that has been a place of worship for local people since before the birth of Christ.

In the time of the Celts the land stood at the heart of the tribe's culture and way of life. Marked by standing stones it was a place of worship attracting druids from throughout the West of Scotland.

This was to change with the arrival from Ireland of St Mahew, reputedly a disciple of St Patrick. The saint made for the site of pagan worship and, ignoring the warriors, druids and obvious danger, cut the sign of the cross into the face of the central stone. This signalled the arrival of the word of God and of His presence among the people. His actions marked the death of an old religion and heralded a new way of living that survives almost fifteen hundred years later.

Mounted on a piece of wood, the stone bearing the mark of St Mahew stands in the doorway of the small church that has taken his name. The history of this land is marked by periods of prosperity and ruin similar to those experienced by most churches in Scotland. As the centuries passed the modest little cill, or church, survived in various forms. St Mahew may have gone but his message and example live on.

In the Middle Ages the small chapel was a major landmark in the area and local rumour suggests that King Robert the Bruce may have knelt in prayer beneath its thatched roof.

The chapel came under the auspices of a Roger Cochrane in 1329 and eventually into the hands of the Napier family – a connection which is still evident. During the fourteenth century the Napiers added to their estates the half lands of Kilmahew. The family controlled the lands for the next four hundred years.

Before the arrival of the Napiers, the cill had fallen into disrepair. In the fifteenth century, Duncan Napier funded its renovation for the spiritual needs of the people. By May 1467 the cill was rebuilt and consecrated by George Lawder,

The picturesque St Mahew's church

St Mahew's church

floorboards. Reports of the poor flooring were confirmed during a later refurbishment which revealed a number of Charles II coins which had fallen through the numerous cracks.

The year 1744 was to end another chapter of local history with the decline of the Napiers. The family and their castle fell into ruin and their lands were sold on to recoup debts. The demise of the family signalled the passing of an old way of life. The Industrial Revolution saw Glasgow grow and change while neighbouring Dumbarton developed with the arrival of new industries.

With the closure of the school in 1846, the chapel fell into a state of neglect and disrepair until 1948 when it again came under the care of the Catholic Church and the Archdiocese of Glasgow. Predictably the new owners sanctioned the complete restoration of the building as a church and began to reconstruct the ancient chapel.

This restoration work was to unearth further evidence of the proud past, revealing tombs dating as far back as the ninth century and the ancient standing stone bearing the sign of the cross. Finally in May 1955 Mass was again celebrated in the Church – the first for more than four hundred years.

Bishop of Argyll. The ceremony saw the chapel officially recognised as a church, confirming its place at the heart of the local people.

The next major upheaval was the coming of the Reformation. The changes this period forced upon the Church are well documented and were felt in the ancient chapel. As the liturgy changed and priests were driven into hiding the chapel of St Mahew became a 'preaching station' for the new faith. A reader conducted worship in the chapel and at one point it was almost chosen as the parish church for the area. This idea was ruled out and the chapel became the local schoolhouse, remaining so from 1640 until 1846.

Today the old Session Records give some idea as to the state of the building, commenting on its crumbling structure and weak

Gentle haven

The ancient cill of St Mahew stands as one of the most beautiful small churches in Scotland. Situated off the main road leading through Cardross village the building and its surrrounds lie in a peaceful haven. This external beauty is matched by the beautiful interior.

The Rood Loft which stands above the altar, backed by deep blue and golden stars, tells some of the proud history of the church. A Latin inscription reads:

> Donald, Archbishop of Glasgow, caused this venerable church of St Mahew to be restored after it had fallen into ruin in the passing of the years, and piously he embellished it in the year of Our Lord, 1955.

Above are the figures of Our Lady and Saint John and six coats of arms. First is the Papal badge of Pope Paul II, the coats of Bishop Andrew Muirhead of Glasgow and Bishop George Lawder – instrumental in the original consecration in 1467.

In reference to the most recent restoration in 1955 are the arms of Pope Pius XII, Archbishop Donald Campbell of Glasgow and Bishop Kenneth Grant of Argyll and the Isles. Linking the two clusters of shields is the coat of arms of Duncan Napier of Kilmahew, whose patronage ensured the cill's relevance in the spiritual lives of the local people. At the entrance to the church is the simple stone, marked by St Mahew – the founding rock on which this community has thrived.

The stone on which St Mahew carved the cross of Christ

St Mahew's church interior

RIOT IN ST GILES CATHEDRAL

WHEN KING JAMES VI DIED in March 1625, his son was proclaimed King and became Charles I. During his reign the dispute between the opposing Protestant factions in the country showed no signs of diminishing. The role which the new monarch performed in this civil war hastened his own destruction.

Within weeks of assuming the throne Charles made public his strong support for Episcopalianism by attempting to recover possession of Presbyterian Church lands and benefit the Episcopal Church. Although such actions were in keeping with the statutes which had established the Episcopalian system in Scotland, it did produce dissent. As a further provocative measure, Charles introduced Anglican liturgical innovations into the worship.

The King's return to Scotland in 1633 precipitated a collision between the monarch and the Presbyterianism of his subjects. His fellow countrymen were to be further enraged by the trial of Lord Balmerino for treason. His crime was simply to possess a petition against the royal measures and when Charles engaged in quarrels with the English Parliament this added to the sense of distance from their new ruler. The immediate cause of the escalating dispute was the decision to introduce a set liturgy into the public worship.

His strategy in bringing this measure forward differed from that of his father, who merely regarded it as a tactic to entrench the power of the monarchy. Charles, in contrast, held the enhancement of Episcopalianism as central to his religious convictions. It was inevitable that confrontation would follow and it did on 23 July 1637.

In Edinburgh the Presbyterian leaders had been stirring up their followers and during the inauguration of the new liturgy St Giles Cathedral was crowded. The Archbishops of St Andrews and Glasgow were present in support of the Episcopalian cause and the Presbyterians were represented by a handful of ministers. A full scale riot ensued when the Presbyterians smashed the windows of the church and assailed the Episcopalians with insults and abusive language. One of the bishops was grabbed by a group of women and rolled in the mire.

When no action was taken against the rioters it reinforced the impression that the country was stubbornly Presbyterian and would not countenance the imposition of unwanted doctrine from a distant King. This stance resulted in the strengthening of Presbyterian power and a new covenant was constructed. It was called the National Covenant and was ordered to be read in every Kirk in the kingdom.

Under the threat of excommunication and eternal damnation the populace were instructed to add their names to this document which railed against 'Popery, Prelacy, and all their supporters and adherents'. The subscribers to the covenant were whipped up into a frenzy and declared Catholics and Episcopalians to be criminals outside the protection of the law.

Alarmed by this storm of protest Charles attempted to calm the Scots by offering to withdraw the unpopular service-book and suspend the jurisdiction of the Episcopal courts. The General Assembly, adopting the role of spokesman for the Scottish people, would countenance no compromise. They met at Glasgow in 1638 and passed a motion abolishing not only the King's liturgy and canons, but Episcopacy itself. Despite protests from Scotland's bishops, and the Royal Commissioners' Act declaring the Assembly dissolved, they confirmed their resolution the following year.

Meanwhile, the Covenanters, after defending their own borders, gathered a substantial army, crossed the Tweed and marched into England. The opposition of the English Parliament to the Royal decrees reinforced the Covenanters in their stance and they were further supported by the actions of the Parliament in producing the Grand Remonstrance, which listed grievances against Charles I and which precipitated the raising of the Royal Standard at Nottingham, and the inevitable outbreak of the Civil War.

Victory

The Scottish Covenanters sided with the popular party in the English Parliament and entered into the Solemn League and Covenant in 1643. One of the conditions of this alliance was the raising of a new Scottish army, which marched into England in the winter of 1644 and helped to secure the victory of Marston Moor.

The efforts of Montrose in Scotland failed to help the Royal cause and Charles in desperation turned to the Presbyterians who, afraid of provoking the wrath of their southern neighbours, handed him over to the English Parliament.

Despite this King Charles would not capitulate and this set in motion a chain of events which would culminate in his trial and execution. A force of his supporters, headed by the Duke of Hamilton, crossed the Border in 1648, but were defeated by Oliver Cromwell's Parliamentary troops.

This was part of a pattern of victories for Cromwell leading to his emergence as a powerful force in British life. It would also herald a new onslaught on the Catholic faith and its practitioners, particularly in Ireland.

ST COLUMBA

LYING SOUTH OF SKYE and west of the mainland, the island of Canna is reached by catching the ferry from Mallaig. There are two islands, Canna and Sanday. Sanday, a rocky stretch of land rising from the sea in the harbour, is regarded by most as a part of Canna and can be reached by a footbridge or by walking across the bay at low tide. The craggy sides of the isle of Rhum look down on the island and Skye and Barra can be seen from the bay.

St Columba's before refurbishment

As in all of Scotland's Western Isles, the Vikings played an important part in Canna's history. There are many Norse words among its place names.

Arriving in Scotland in 563, St Columba established the monastery on Iona, which was pivotal in the conversion of the Picts, Scots and the people of what is now the North of England. His exile in the Highlands and Islands, between 563 and 597, laid the foundation of a strong Christian tradition and his example inspired the missionaries who followed him.

Throughout Columba's story there is reference to *Hinba*, a settlement which was used as a place of retreat by the saint. The late Dr John Lorne Campbell argues the case for Canna being Hinba, citing evidence of a pre-Columba settlement on the isle, the accessibility of the harbour and the many coincidences that arise between descriptions of Hinba and Canna.

Around 793 the people of Scotland had their first experience of a Viking raiding party – the beginning of two hundred years of rape, pillage and murder committed by the Norse invaders. The Hebridean isles were seen as ripe for plunder, mainly because of the efforts of Columba and his followers, who established churches and monasteries containing many valuable relics. The monastery at Iona was besieged and burned on several occasions, including one attack which left 68 people dead. Canna, a place of retreat and prayer for the Celtic Saint, was used as a staging point for many of the Viking raids.

The Vikings ruled the Hebrides for four centuries and their influence is visible on Canna in the shape of nine unexcavated Viking burial mounds, one of which is thought to contain a longboat. The site is one of many ruins that continue to fascinate scholars.

One of the many Celtic crosses

At an almost unreachable point on a southern ledge of the island are the ruins of a Columban nunnery dating before the tenth century. On top of a large rock, north of the bay, is evidence of an old castle called 'the prison'. As legend has it, one of Canna's ancient rulers imprisoned his young wife in a fit of jealousy and held her there until she died. On the edge of the bay, on the site of the pre-Highland Clearance village of Keill, stands a remarkably well-preserved Celtic cross, another clue to the island's enduring Christian tradition. Overlooking the boundaries of the old village, rising from the peak of a nearby hill, is the island's punishment stone. In times past criminals would have their thumb jammed into a small hole in the face of the stone and be left alone with their conscience and the elements.

The persecution which occurred during the Reformation was to inspire heroics from the island missionaries. An appeal was made to the Irish Franciscan College of St Antony of Padua, Louvain, at a time when there were no priests left in the Highlands and Islands and not one Gaelic-speaking seminarian in any of the exiled Scots colleges. Inspired by the example of St Columba, the Irishmen were to ensure that Catholicism survived in the islands, saying Mass and administering the sacraments in the shadow of capture and imprisonment.

Islanders outside St Columba's before renovation

Following the 1745 uprising Alexander MacDonald, Bailie of Canna, wrote one of the first books to contain Gaelic poems and songs, making him one of the island's most important historical figures and marking him out as a Jacobite in the eyes of the Crown. MacDonald was on the run until 1747 and his infamy attracted enemies to the island.

In April 1746 a party of eighty troops landed, first with the intention of stealing cattle but soon turning to rape and murder. A fifty-year-old woman, who was ill and pregnant, survived an assault

New stained glass window   *St Columba's after renovation*

discovered that the troop-ship *Queen Mary* had collided with a destroyer. The periscopes of enemy subs often popped their heads above the water and two islanders saw a U-boat docked on a remote Canna shore, stocking up with fresh water from a stream.

Co-owning the island with her husband Dr John Lorne Campbell, Mrs Campbell entrusted its care to the National Trust for Scotland, thus ensuring safe patronage for the island's residents, who live with the same determination and commitment as their forefathers. It will guarantee the island's status as a peaceful sanctuary, while preserving it as one of Scotland's national treasures.

On the feast day of St Columba 9 June 2001, residents and friends gathered to celebrate the rededication of their church. The event was of special significance as it marked the end of almost four years' work on the building. It celebrated a return to former glory for the old church which was built before 1740 and has served the islanders for more than two centuries.

Bishop Ian Murray's first official visit to Canna

only later to lose both her life and the child. Other island women were forced into the hills until the party left. Raiding and harassment became a feature of Canna life but the islanders never betrayed their faith or their Jacobite beliefs.

In recent times the island has had more than its fair share of excitement, as its owner, Margaret Fay Shaw Campbell, tells in her autobiography *From the Alleghenies to the Hebrides*. The Second World War brought further tragedy as many of the island's men were lost in the conflict. War was to visit Canna in a visible form after two trawlers were sunk by a German submarine not far from the bay. The survivors were cared for by the islanders and the bodies of the victims were washed ashore during the following days.

Margaret Campbell also recounts the tragic sight of a rocky cove on Sanday filled with the blue caps of navymen. The islanders later

St Columba's had fallen into disrepair when in 1998 snow began to fall inside the church through a hole in the roof and repairing the slates for the umpteenth time, the islanders decided that a more permanent solution was needed.

Murdo Jack, the island's master builder, volunteered to take on the job of rebuilding. Renovation was no mean feat considering the extent of the repairs. The undertaking is even more remarkable considering that Murdo is the island's only non-Catholic resident.

Under his guidance each of the islanders helped in rebuilding the church while friends from the mainland and beyond have contributed.

In August 1998 the fund raised almost £6000 and other donations boosted the total to £19,000. Parishioners of Morar and Mallaig donated chairs for the church engraved with their names.

Expert artist Martin Farrelly donated his talent designing and fitting the stained-glass windows. Other benefactors included Archbishop Keith Patrick O'Brien, The Craigmyle Trust and the island's patron and matriarch, Mrs Margaret Fay Shaw Campbell of Canna.

The church was officially opened on St Columba's feast day by Bishop Ian Murray during his first visit to Canna, which was also the first time he had dedicated a church.

'I hadn't realised just how far off the mainland the island is,' said Bishop Murray. *'And it was a beautiful day when we got there. I was taken with the church, it was a great moment of achievement for the people of Canna and is as much about community building and the building of the Church as a whole as it was about building a church.'*

CHARLES II AND JAMES II

WHEN CHARLES II WAS RESTORED to the throne in May 1660, the Catholic community in Scotland had already experienced decades of severe prejudice. The monarch, although brought up by his father as a Protestant, was to prove closer to Catholicism. When he lived in Paris with his mother his experiences were not entirely alien to the Catholic tradition.

Henrietta Maria would take her sons to visit the Carmelite nuns so they might be converted to the faith. In the Declaration of Breda, Charles had pledged to guarantee liberty of conscience to all his subjects. The conversion to Catholicism of his brother James years afterwards helped him to adopt a benevolent view of his Catholic subjects.

Unfortunately this enlightened attitude did not extend very far into the heart of the religious establishment in Scotland. Although the King had abolished the Presbyterian form of church government by a 1662 Act of Parliament and restored the Episcopalian system, acts such as the public burning of the Pope in effigy by students of Edinburgh College were permitted and even actively encouraged.

Severe measures were taken against Catholic families in the north of Scotland, such as the Gordons of Carmellie and Littlemill and the Grants of Ballindalloch, all of whom were charged with harbouring priests and attending Catholic Mass. Due to such action, taking stock of the faithful in the country was as difficult to do as it was depressing to contemplate. A census in 1681 showed that the number of communicants who 14,000 and of these 12,000 belonged to the Highlands and Islands. The remoteness of these areas from the centre of government and the long arm of the penal laws offset the effectiveness of depressing the Catholic population.

Galloway possessed 550 adherents, Glasgow and the neighbouring areas 50; in Forfarshire 72; in Aberdeenshire 450; in Banffshire, 1000 and in Morayshire, 28. The report commended the fidelity of laity and clergy, but concluded that the opportunity of their hearing Mass more than three times a year could only be achieved by hazardous travel.

The death of King Charles II in February 1685 and the succession of his brother James, Duke of York, was an event which would have far-reaching consequences for the Catholics of Scotland. James II was a Catholic convert and in 1673 had married the Catholic princess Mary Beatrix of Este.

Almost immediately James suspended the penal statutes against Catholics. During the residence of James in Edinburgh as Duke of York, the Catholic service had been celebrated in the Palace of Holyrood. From his privy purse two hundred pounds a year was given for the Chapel Royal, the mission in the Highlands, the Jesuit missionaries and the Scots Colleges at Douai, Paris and Rome. Clearly, while the rights of the Established Church in Scotland would be upheld, liberty of conscience for all religious denominations would be secure. It was not to be.

The outrage of his Presbyterian subjects, fed by the fanatical zeal of the preachers, sparked a backlash. James abandoned his crown to William of Orange, the husband of his eldest daughter Mary. The Catholics of Scotland were thus allowed only a brief respite from persecution, which the accession of James II had gained for them.

CILLE BHARRA (CHURCH OF ST BARR)

APPROACHING BY FERRY it is easy to see why the island of Barra has been described as the most beautiful of the Western Isles.

As the boat cuts down from South Uist you bypass the rocky outcrops of Gighay and Hellisay. Rising from the water shrouded in mist, they look almost prehistoric and it is not surprising to discover that the rocks which make up the islands are among the most ancient in Europe.

Barra, however. is far from being barren or bleak. On a sunny day, its lush green fields, trimmed with stunning golden beaches and green tinted shallows make Barra the jewel in the crown of the Western Isles.

The island has three primary schools and one secondary, with two parishes and a total of five Catholic churches. It is attached to the neighbouring isle of Vatersay by a man-made rock causeway. The combined population of around one thousand has been known to double in the summer as visitors flock to the island, but as in the past, the main industry is fishing and boats leave every week carrying produce to Spain and France. The annual fisherman's Mass is one of the highlights of the Catholic calendar and the life of the Church is interwoven with that of the people.

Man has been settled on Barra since prehistoric times. Evidence remains of ancient hill forts and standing stones are still visible.

The arrival of St Columba in Iona in around 563 heralded the advent of Christianity. Fifty years later the missionaries he inspired brought the Word to Barra. Among those missionaries was St Brendan the Voyager. Brendan is credited with discovering America, one thousand years before Columbus and even before the Vikings, in around 530–560. He and a party of missionaries left Ireland 'going wherever the wind took them.'

Early in their travels one brother monk died, forcing Brendan to land on the west coast of Barra to carry out the funeral. The saint buried his friend, said Mass, stocked up on provisions and left for the north of America, exploring as far down the coast as Florida.

In the centuries that followed, as legend suggests, the island became a base for Viking pirates. This signalled a new era and a dark time for Christian settlements, which were regularly pillaged. Evidence of a number of

Cille Bharra

The bay at St Barr's

The details of St Finbarr's life have been lost but his story shares many similarities with that of St Finbarr of Cork. Both saints have the same feast day, on 27 September, but in Scotland and Ireland the legends surrounding them differ dramatically.

Finbarr's Scots history tells how he was the illegitimate son of a Sutherland nobleman. When the King of Sutherland discovered the indiscretion he decreed that both parties be burned at the stake. Finbarr, still in his mother's womb, called out a warning to the king that he would be punished for such a cruel act. It was obvious to all that the child was special. Later he studied, became a monk, visited Barra, founding the ancient cille and ended his life as a hermit.

New church of St Barr's

St Finbarr's cille has remained a place of worship through the centuries and the present church, Cille Bharra, stands on the original site.

It is this church which reveals the first signs of Viking conversion to the Christian faith. Inside the Cille lies a replica of an ancient stone discovered in the grounds which shows a Celtic Cross and a runic dedication from Steinar, the island's Viking chief, to mark the Christian burial of his daughter Thorgeth.

pagan/Norse graves on the island suggest that the influence of Christianity may have weakened during the first one hundred years of Viking occupation though evidence from the ancient Cille Bharra (Church of St Barr), founded by St Finbarr of Barra in the early seventh century, shows this to have been temporary.

The ancient church of Cille Bharra

The Reformation was the next big test of the strength of the island's faith. Although there is evidence that Macneil of Barra, the island chief, converted to Protestantism, most of the islanders remained faithful to their Catholic heritage. The new local ministers tended to have a rough time on the island and in 1609 the brigand, Macdonald of Benbecula, murdered the minister John Macneill. No replacement was appointed.

Throughout this period the islanders clung to their traditions and devotion to St Finbarr flourished in secret. The coming of the Irish Franciscan missionaries reaffirmed the islanders' beliefs as they delivered the Sacraments and said Mass secretly in barns or in fields.

The sanctuary lamps have never been extinguished in Barra and the Catholic faith has survived. One missionary who visited the isle in 1632 said that the people were 'very devout and very desirous of learning and Catholic instruction.'

What evidence is there that St Brendan had visited Barra? People did not have books to record their stories, but they did have songs and a tradition of story-telling passed down through the generations by word of mouth. People seek evidence to prove the stories, but they cannot prove they are untrue.

The pirate clan

In 1427, Alexander of Islay, Lord of the Isles, gave the island of Barra and land in South Uist to Gill-Adhamnain, the son of Roderick Macneil. This established the name of Macneil at the helm of the isle and placed the Macneils firmly in the annals of Scots history. Their traditional home is the first sight that meets visitors to the island. Sitting in the centre of Barra harbour, surrounded by water, is the family home, Kisimul Castle. With its own supply of fresh water, from a well in the rock on which it was built, the castle was soon known as one of the most impregnable keeps in the country.

In ancient times the Macneils had a reputation as a formidable pirate force, owning one of the best boats in the Isles, built using skills learnt from the Vikings. Their vessel was called the Birlinn and its speed was legendary. Raiding merchant ships, the Macneils brought some of the finest wines and silks back to the island, so much in fact that it became a standing joke that even the horses drank wine on Barra. This tradition of the Macneils taking to water has lasted through the centuries.

When Bonnie Prince Charlie came over in 1745 he landed on Eriskay, recruiting a Macneil who was the chief's personal piper to steer him there. The chief was away on business at the time, which proved to be quite fortuitous for the Macneils as they missed out on the unsuccessful Jacobite Rebellion. The people of the island may have been sympathetic to the Jacobite cause but their lack of involvement saved them from the persecution of the clans following defeat.

Inside the ancient church of Cille Bharra

The Macneil family history has included some unscrupulous characters, notably Marion of the Heads. Marion resided in Kisimul Castle in 1427 with her son Ruari. Following the death of her husband she had both her stepsons beheaded in Vatersay Bay to ensure Ruari's place as chief. The act gave Marion a taste for 'chops' and beheadings became commonplace on the island while she held the throne. Also in Vatersay Bay is a cluster of rocks known as 'the prison' where Marion kept servants that were too old or sick to work. They drowned as the high tides rolled in.

The family history is not all bad. The clan has given Scotland some of its finest and bravest priests. Among them was Fr John Macneil, born in 1880 and among the first to volunteer for the Cameron Highlanders when war broke out in 1914. He became a legend in battle, a talisman on the front line who charged in the thick of the fight and won a Military Cross and later the award of the Bar. He was wounded in an attack on Paschendaele Ridge but returned to service after his recovery and saw the end of the war as chaplain on HMS *Bellerophon*. Returning to Scotland, he founded Our Lady of Sorrows in Daliburgh and went on to serve the parish of Morar with distinction.

AFTER THE BATTLE OF THE BOYNE

THE ABANDONMENT OF THE CROWN by James II to William of Orange was followed by an equally disastrous attempt to regain it at the Battle of the Boyne on 11 July 1690.

The Scottish Catholics were once again exposed to the full blast of the storm that had swept James from the throne. Mobs paraded through the streets of Edinburgh demanding the death of the two chief ministers, the Chancellor Perth and his brother, the Earl of Melfort, Secretary of State. The gates of Holyrood Palace were forced, the guards murdered and the chapel, schools and library were rifled and their contents publicly burnt. The intruders then proceeded into the town, plundering and burning the houses of Catholics.

It was becoming clear, despite the assurances of King William III that the Catholics of Great Britain would continue to enjoy royal protection, nothing would be been done to moderate the violence against them. In 1699 the Duke of Gordon was seized in his own house in Edinburgh where Mass was being celebrated by a gathering of Catholics. The Duke was imprisoned for two weeks and was only liberated after issuing a humble apology to the Privy Council.

In May 1700 a new and severe Act of Parliament was passed, assigning a reward of five hundred merks for the detection of every priest or Jesuit and ordering the banishment of all such persons, on pain of death, if they returned to Scotland.

Catholics were, by the same statute, declared incapable of inheriting property, or of educating their children. It was the increased ferocity of this legal discrimination that turned the Holy See to the necessity of providing a facility for the ordination of priests and placing them under an episcopal superior.

The king died in March 1702, after a reign of 14 years. Although historical revisionism makes the case that William displayed a level of indulgence towards his English Catholic subjects, Scotland and Ireland were not treated so favourably. The penal statutes were enforced in Scotland with even more severity than before.

The accession of Anne, the sister-in-law of William and younger daughter of James II, brought little relief to the Scottish Catholics. The reign of the last of the Stuarts was marked by an event fraught with crucial consequence for Scotland – the Union of Parliaments in 1707.

A special statute was passed providing for the maintenance and establishment of the Presbyterian system in Scotland. Tolerance was at the same time guaranteed to members of the Episcopal communion though, in fact, liberty of conscience and worship was denied to those of the Catholic faith.

In the early eighteenth century a report by a Cardinal Noris stated that the object of the government was the total extermination of the Catholic religion throughout the country. It was forbidden to employ Catholics in domestic service and every effort was made to apprehend and convict as many priests as possible.

In the midst of such persecution converts were being added to the Church. This only increased the jealousy of Protestant ministers, who in 1710 lobbied for the stronger enforcement of the penal laws. The first Jacobite rising five years later provoked fresh sufferings for the Catholics. Many priests were imprisoned and banished.

Indeed, a report of Bishop Gordon, sent in 1716, stated that Catholics were in danger of total annihilation and the faith was on the verge of floundering completely.

The General Assembly of 1721 stated:

> 'The great matter we have before us, is the terrible growth of Popery in the north. We met on that committee from three to seven this night. The accounts are most lamentable – bishops, priests, and Jesuits are exercising openly their functions. Seminaries and schools are openly set up and multitudes sent abroad and coming home from Popish seminaries every three or four months.'

ARISAIG

THE WHITE SANDS OF MORAR are one of the most beautiful features of the Western Highlands. Touched by the light blue and green waters between the Sound of Sleat and the Sound of Arisaig, the village bay looks more Caribbean than Scottish.

The village is also known as the Gateway to the Western Isles and is part of a territory steeped in Catholic history.

The persecution on the ground was bolstered by Acts of Parliament, one of which even went so far as to abolish the name of MacGregor.

Despite this, many of the clans tried to live in some sort of harmony with the Crown. Turning their backs on the south, they hoped to be left alone. But Government officials, tax collectors and English and Scots Lowland soldiers continued to harass the people. This was the backdrop to the rebellions of 1715 and 1745, the more famous of these being the Forty-Five.

Arisaig was the landing point for Charles Edward Stuart in 1745 and the people suffered terribly in the wake of his defeat at Culloden in April 1746.

On that day less than 5000 exhausted and half-starved Highland men faced an army, double in size, on open ground which no officer but Charles believed could be defended. Following the battle, the Government force, made up of English, Lowland and Campbell troops, passed over the field of battle bayoneting the wounded. More than 1000 Jacobites died at Culloden that day and, in the persecution that followed, approximately 120 were executed and 1150 transported to America as slaves, while the fate of 700 men, women and children remains unknown.

Defeat also saw the suppression of the Clans pursued with vigour by 'Butcher' Cumberland.

The Act for the Pacification of the Highlands in 1747 was aimed at shattering the infrastructure of the clans, outlawing their traditions and stripping the clan chiefs of their power. Massacres were still regarded as a suitable way of addressing the Highland problem, with one officer on record as considering the slaughter of the entire MacPherson clan as a solution to Highland disturbances.

The new church of St Mary's

The old Catholic Church and graveyard in Arisaig

Many Catholic priests made the journey into exile with their people and laid the foundations of a Catholic Church which would gradually flourish. Today in Nova Scotia, thriving parishes in places such as New Glasgow, Lismore and Arisaig are a vital part of the Diocese of Antigonish and of the wider Canadian Catholic Church. The founding bishops of that diocese, William Fraser and Colin F MacKinnon, were Scots and they, together with their people, have ensured that good was borne from the ashes of their lives in Scotland.

ST MARY'S CHURCH

THE STRUCTURE OF ST MARY'S Church in Arisaig reflects the strength of the Catholic faith in this coastal area, which was a landing point for the monks from the abbey on Iona who first brought Christianity to Scotland. The graveyard beside the old church is a resting place for some of those early missionaries.

Following the Reformation, Arisaig was revived as a Catholic enclave. In 1677 Alexander Leslie, the Papal representative appointed to assess the state of Scotland more than one hundred years after the Reformation, noted that the local population of Arisaig was still Catholic. Arisaig became the mission station serving the Western Highland region. It was also the location for a Catholic school which sent young Highlanders abroad to Scots Colleges.

As the Church embarked on its programme of church building, the community at Arisaig received a new place of worship in the shape of St Mary's, opened in 1849. Inside the church is a clock

The village at Arisaig still bears the scars of this 'solution'. A walk around the surrounding fields reveals the foundations and stones of a once thriving community.

In the 1840s more than 1000 of Arisaig's 1500 inhabitants were 'removed' to make way for the Cheviot sheep, which was considered a far more profitable and less troublesome tenant. Some of the Western Highlanders fled into the wilds, where they struggled to survive. Others were forced into the slums of Glasgow, working as labourers in the growing city. Several thousand, however, were more fortunate and were able to leave for Canada, where they established Nova Scotia and introduced Catholicism to the new community.

dedicated to the Gaelic poet Alasdair MacDonald, a further indicator of the long-standing Catholic, Gaelic and Celtic tradition here.

Arisaig was used as a training centre for commandos during the Second World War, but perhaps the village's greatest claim to fame is that it is the real-life birthplace of one of fiction's most famous characters.

Long John Silver was born in Arisaig in 1853. A skilled craftsman, he travelled to Barra Head to help build the lighthouse there under the supervision of one Robert Stevenson. It was there he met young Robert Louis and clearly made a lasting impression on the boy who later moulded him into one of the world's most famous pirates.

Inside the old Catholic Church in Arisaig (above and right)

AN EXTRAORDINARY PRELATE

FOLLOWING THE CALAMITY of Culloden, the loss was to signal an event of importance for the spread of the faith in Scotland. This was the conversion of a young Edinburgh student who was to become one of the most committed and charismatic prelates ever to oversee the Scottish Church.

George Hay was born of Protestant parents in August 1729 and entered Edinburgh University to study medicine. By the time Charles Edward Stuart landed on the coast of Scotland, Hay had already made significant advances. After his victory at Prestonpans, the Prince requested medical assistance for the wounded. Hay was among those who attended the battlefield and for the following months he observed the Prince's fortunes.

Illness forced him to return to Edinburgh and the defeat at Culloden saw him arrested for taking part in the rebellion and taken prisoner to London. During his captivity he received many visits from a Catholic bookseller called Meighan and it was through this friendship that he first acquired knowledge of Catholic doctrine.

On 21 December 1748, not long after his return to Scotland, he made his profession of the Catholic faith. The 20-year-old convert soon resumed his studies but under the penal laws was barred from obtaining his diploma of doctor of medicine. He accepted the appointment of surgeon on a vessel and whilst abroad formed a friendship with Bishop Challoner. This prelate recognised the abilities of the young physician and inspired him to pursue theological studies. From this meeting Hay decided to undertake a new vocation.

When his work as ship's surgeon was terminated he made his way to the Scots College in Rome and after eight years of study was ordained as a priest on 2 April 1758.

Leaving Rome to begin work in Scotland, he was assigned to the extensive district of Rathven, but was soon moved to Preshome, where his ancestor had been minister two centuries before.

Towards the close of 1767, Bishop Grant, conscious of his failing powers, proposed the appointment of Hay as coadjutor. This was granted and on Trinity Sunday, 1769, he received the Episcopal consecration at Scalan. The new prelate set up his residence in Edinburgh. The work undertaken by Bishop Hay was substantial. For more than half a century he braved the dire consequences of discrimination and draconian penal laws, undergoing an ordeal which seems unbelievable today.

After his consecration he proposed a memorial on behalf of the persecuted inhabitants of South Uist, where the laird, himself an apostate Catholic, had tried to force nearly two hundred families to abandon the faith of their fathers. The laird's first move was to coerce Catholic children to attend Protestant schools. It was said that during Lent of 1770 attempts were made to force them to eat meat.

Deprived

Catholic parents withdrew their children from the schools while the laird assembled all his tenants ordering them to sign a declaration renouncing their religion or be deprived of their holdings. The people refused to comply with the demand and declared their readiness to beg in the streets rather than deny their birthright. Disarmed by the zeal of his tenants the laird pledged to leave them be, provided they consent to their children being brought up as Protestants.

All efforts having proved fruitless, the solution to the problem seemed clear – emigration. The call came from Bishop Hay: an appeal for money to defray the cost of transporting the emigrants to America. Subscriptions poured in and his letter written on 10 July 1772 expressed the hope that this exodus of Scottish Catholics might have at least one good result – the spread of the Catholic faith in distant lands.

EILEAN BAN SEMINARY

THE STORM THAT BLEW ACROSS Scotland's social landscape in 1560 left the Catholic Church on its knees. The measures taken by the Government left the Church reliant on foreign missionaries and a small number of native priests who were educated overseas. The Catholic heirarchy recognised the urgent need for native priests, 'Heather priests', who would better understand the needs of their flock and be prepared for the hard life on the Mission. A priest trained in Scotland would be less likely, in theory, to suffer a mental, physical or spiritual collapse while on the run. The location for such an illegal seminary would have to be carefully chosen in a place where the majority of local people would be sympathetic.

The seminary on Eilean Ban (the Fair Isle) on Loch Morar was opened in 1714. It was the first seminary to be opened in the British Isles after the Reformation and its location was perfect. The island had already been used, without any adverse consequences, as a meeting place for the Western Highland missionaries. However the timing of the opening of the college could not have been more unfortunate.

The 1715 Jacobite Rising brought down the wrath of the Government on the area. Following the Jacobite defeat the college was abandoned as troops flooded the area. Catholicism had long been seen as a symbol of the rebellion and priests were hunted as traitors.

In 1729, the Catholic Church underwent serious changes as the Mission divided into two Vicariates – Highland and Lowland. Highland and Lowland Scotland were like two separate countries and the Church recognised that change was needed to better serve the people. Evidence of the divide between the two peoples was perhaps best seen across the country at the hidden seminary in Scalan. The Highland and Lowland students had split into two camps divided by language, tradition and culture.

The re-opening of the seminary on Eilean Ban in 1732, this time catering specifically for Highland students, seemed the most logical way to solve the problem. In 1738 the college closed again, this time due to financial difficulties.

The poverty of the Mission at that point was crushing and, starved of funds from Rome, the Church was at breaking point. Although the Scottish Church would survive, this heralded the end for the island seminary.

Loch Morar and surrounding countryside

The interior of Our Lady of Perpetual Succour and St Cumin

Bishop Hugh was 47. After a time of hiding out in the neighbouring area the bishop fled to France where he remained until 1749.

Today, the only remaining clues as to the island's important history are the outlines of the seminary buildings and the base of the wall which surrounded Bishop MacDonald's beloved garden.

BLESSED MORAR

Blessed Morar must rank as one of the most visually stunning places in the Western Highlands. Hemmed in by the hills and mountains, Loch Morar and its surrounding coastline is both tranquil and breathtaking. This beautiful scenery is the location for an equally beautiful church.

Following the Jacobite defeat at Culloden in 1746 the island again became a place of refuge. After the closure of the seminary, Bishop Hugh MacDonald had remained at his house and he was soon joined by refugees from Culloden including Simon, Lord Lovat and his brother the Laird of Morar. In June 1746 the Argyllshire Government Militia, led by Major-General Campbell, sailed from Tobermory to flush out the rebels. They spread themselves on the banks of the loch and opened fire on the island. Most escaped although the bishop's chapel and house were gutted and hundreds of years of Catholic archives went up in smoke.

In statements made by the soldiers at the time great play is made of their pursuit of the bishop, although no mention appears within the reports of their gallantry of the fact that Lord Lovat was 80 while

The old church at Bracarina

Vestments used by a chaplain to Bonnie Prince Charlie's army

Rev Ronald McDonald's head stone

The present day church of Our Lady of Perpetual Succour and St Cumin

here one priest would serve an area of several hundred miles. Travelling on foot and by boat to the surrounding villages he would stay with his flock, relying on their hospitality to survive. Evidence of this tradition remains today with the parish priest calling from time to time on local fishermen to take him to the remote island churches.

With the passing of the Catholic Relief Bill in 1793, which allowed Catholics to practise their faith freely, it seemed only right that Morar be chosen as the site for a new church. The parish priest at that time was Ranald MacDonell, who had served the Morar Mission since 1782. He established the area's first permanent parish, building a priest's house and eventually a new church in nearby Bracarina in 1832.

Within thirty years, widespread improvements had been made in the locale as Lord Lovat began on a programme of renovation. A new Morar Lodge was completed in 1878 and the laird immediately set in motion plans for a new church to replace the crumbling old building. But Lord Lovat died suddenly in 1887 before the church was completed. His widow, Lady Lovat, was determined to realise his dream and on 2 May 1889 the church of Our Lady and St Cumin was finally opened.

Inside and around the church evidence remains of the region's long-standing Catholic tradition. Vestments used by a chaplain serving in Bonnie Prince Charlie's Jacobite army in 1745 hang in a glass case near a chalice dating back to 1658, which was used by the Dominican missionary, Fr Vincent Morrison.

The small present-day Catholic community is as active in supporting the Church, at parish and national level, as its predecessors.

Driving out from Morar village you follow the road down on to the lochside where you are greeted by the sight of the church of Our Lady of Perpetual Succour and St Cumin. With its turret rising from the side of the building, the church looks as though it has been transferred on to the landscape from a storybook. This peaceful place was also an ancient haven for outlawed Catholic priests after the Reformation. It has long been regarded as a sacred place, so much so that it is known as *Blessed Morar*.

In post-Reformation times the Catholic population was protected by three powerful families – Clans Donald, MacDonald of Glengarry and MacDonald of Clanranald. For outlaw priests, whose lives were fraught with danger, Morar provided a rare place of sanctuary. From

DESTRUCTION OF THE CLANS

IN 1720 LAWS HAD BEEN PASSED aimed at controlling the Catholics, particularly in the Highland districts. A report by the bishops in August 1726 gives some details of the campaign carried out by ministers against the Highland Catholics.

The progress of the Catholic Church in the north was opposed by the preachers, who organised bands of soldiers with the purpose of seizing and imprisoning the missionaries and their converts. To overcome the persecution of the Church the bishops brought forward a proposal for the division of Scotland into two vicariates, the Highland and the Lowland districts.

The bishops recommended for the northern vicariate Alexander Grant, who had been a strong advocate and missionary for the Church. The selection was ratified in July the following year by Pope Benedict XIII. The new bishop-designate initially declined to accept the post but the Pope, using all his powers of persuasion, induced him to accept. Unfortunately while in Genoa he fell ill and nothing more was ever heard of him.

Two years later the bishops renewed their quest to install a vicariate in the Highlands perhaps, because in some areas, Catholics were being compelled to attend the Protestant service.

The new nominee for prelate was Hugh MacDonald, son of the laird of Morar, who had been educated at the seminary of Scalan. It was during the vicariate of Bishop MacDonald that Charles Edward Stuart came to the fore.

In the hope of reclaiming the inheritance of his fathers, Charles landed on the coast of Moidart in July 1745, provoking confusion among the new bishop's advisers. They knew that no strategic preparations had been undertaken to secure success, but they could not fail to offer support for his campaign. The Catholic Highlanders rallied to the Prince, following him to Edinburgh, where he spent the winter preparing for his battle against the Government forces.

Despite an early success at Prestonpans, April 1746 saw the disastrous battle of Culloden and the end to the claims of the Stuarts to the throne. The hopes of the Stuarts being dashed, Henry Benedict, second son of James III, was named Cardinal by Pope Benedict XIV in July of 1747.

If conditions for Highland Catholics were difficult before the Hanoverian army's victory at Culloden they were disastrous following it. More than one thousand people were transported to America, the Highland clans were destroyed and dispersed, Catholic chapels were decimated and the seminary at Scalan plundered and put to the torch. The Catholic people and their priests were persecuted with renewed vigour.

To mitigate these acts Benedict XIV urged Charles Emmanuel III, King of Sardinia, to intercede with the British Government on behalf of the persecuted Catholics of Scotland. Because of his connection with the clans Bishop MacDonald was singled out for close attention and to escape capture he fled to Paris.

Returning in 1749 and with the help and support of the Laird of Leuchars' sister, Bishop MacDonald, using the name Mr Brown, proved adept at ministering to his people for several years. From a report he sent in 1755 we learn he was seized by Government agents and only released from prison upon the payment of a substantial sum.

In 1756, his trial took place before the High Court of Justiciary at Edinburgh and on 1 March, as a punishment for his refusal to 'purge himself of Popery' he was sentenced to lifelong banishment from Scotland under pain of death if he ever returned.

Despite this penalty, Bishop MacDonald continued to perform his duties in the Highlands, probably with the covert compliance of the authorities, until his death there in March 1773.

ST MARY'S CHURCH – BLAIRS

BLAIRS COLLEGE IN ABERDEEN was closed in 1986, more than 150 years after it was founded for the education of young Catholic boys who wanted to become priests. In that time hundreds had entered the seminary including four of Scotland's Hierarchy, namely Archbishop Mario Conti of Glasgow, Bishop Ian Murray of Argyll and the Isles, Bishop Vincent Logan of Dunkeld and Bishop Joseph Devine of Motherwell. The late Cardinal Thomas Winning and Bishop Maurice Taylor of Galloway went to Blairs for their philosophy years, entering after their schooldays were complete. Blairs was an important institution for the Catholic Church in Scotland.

In 1829 local landowner John Menzies of Pitfodels donated his mansion to the Catholic Church along with 1000 acres and thus Blairs was founded. Menzies' portrait is in the Blairs museum with the college in the background and the deeds to the property at his side. The name of St Mary's, Blairs, can clearly be seen.

The Deacon who oversees the running of the St Mary's parish along with the chapel trust and the museum, explained:

'When John Menzies originally donated his mansion it was not big enough for the number of boys who wished to attend so an extension was completed in 1829. Much of the finance came from the landed gentry who sent their sons here thus subsidising the education of the others. The standard was high, preparing the students for the seminaries in France, Spain, Italy and Germany.

The museum and the chapel are part of Scotland's heritage. It represents both the survival and revival of the Catholic Church in Scotland. At its peak there would have been nearly 200 boys living and studying at the college.'

It is planned to convert the complex around the museum and chapel into the 'Gleneagles of the North', with a luxury hotel complex consisting of leisure, equestrian and conference centres. The atmosphere of the college remains and although many of the buildings are now derelict, it is not difficult to picture its former glory. The walled garden overlooked by the original mansion is standing and may be part of the new complex. The chapel inside the mansion was later converted to a theatre, for performances by the seminarians.

Blairs College building (nineteenth-twentieth century) with the chapel, now St Mary's Church, on the left

The magnificent interior of the church at Blairs, which is now the parish church

Inside the museum

legal and medical professions. A website has now been set up for the former students and friends of Blairs. Although the college was closed in 1986 there are plans to refurbish the church. The facilities still owned by the Church are used for many events – it is a favoured venue of the Aberdeen International Youth Festival among other organisations.

THE MUSEUM

The memorabilia on display at Blairs museum are remarkable. Paintings and artefacts dating from the reign of Mary Queen of Scots chart Scotland's history. The collection is on display in the sacristy of the college which is joined to the magnificent chapel. It includes many bequests donated over years as well as items which Blairs acquired from Scottish seminaries. The seminary is part of the heritage collection, derived from seminaries in out of the way places, as well as foreign colleges, which were established to educate priests from the late sixteenth century when it was dangerous to train as a priest. Its history charts the development of Scottish Catholicism.

Entering from the chapel side, the first striking piece is the memorial portrait of Mary Queen of Scots beside one of her as a French princess – a set of which the museum is particularly proud.

The painting of Mary as a captive queen came to Blairs in 1833 having been hidden in a chimney in France during the Revolution. In the archives is the receipt for the carriage of the painting from Leith to Blairs. The museum contains many items associated with

From the start the college was largely self-sufficient because there was a dairy farm in the grounds and it was in an area where fruit and vegetables were plentiful. But this is all in the past.

There is now an active parish of over 200 at St Mary's, as well as the chapel trust and the museum. Blairs is still alive and should not be confined to history.

Many former pupils come back to visit Blairs and tell wonderful stories about their time at the college. Many priests were ordained and the ones who didn't become priests often became involved in Church organisations. Many went abroad and others entered the

the Jacobite uprisings, such as a ring containing a lock of Bonnie Prince Charlie's hair, bequeathed to the college by a family with Jacobite sympathies and a snuff box with an inscription composed by Sir Walter Scott. So many items are available that only a small selection are on display at any one time.

Exhibits such as the priestly garments, the chalices and the monstrances are exquisite and were used by the college, though many date back centuries.

Bishop Hay's chalice is on display as is the monstrance used at Aquhorties, the seminary before Blairs, thus providing a link with the past. There are also chalices and monstrances which were used during the penal times. They are small and could be easily concealed.

There are many beautiful garments with intricate stitching and weaving with gold threads and gem stones sewn into the patterns.

Photographs show the college in the past and there are haunting images of it when it was emptied. The many thousands of books are now on loan to the National Library of Scotland.

The chapel dates from a later time and is built in Gothic-Victorian style with marble-lined walls and oak pews. It is a fitting tribute to Scotland's Catholic past and to those who fought to preserve it. A former seminarian called it 'a chapel worth visiting, a sanctuary worth kneeling before, a home, a history of faith'.

A statue of Our Lady and the Child Jesus

RECLAIMING THE PROPERTY

THE VISIT OF BISHOP HAY to Paris in 1772 was aimed at reclaiming the property and funds of the Scots College at Douai. They had been confiscated by the French Government ten years before, as belonging to the Jesuits. Frequent complaints were made from Scotland that efforts were being made to convert the College into an exclusively Jesuit seminary. The dispute between the Vicars-apostolic and the Society of Jesus was handed over to the Holy See for a decision. By late 1772 no final settlement appeared to have been made.

The Government of Louis XV recognised the justice of the claim and directed the restoration of the property to the Scottish bishops. Following the departure of the Jesuit fathers, the rectorship was held by members of the secular clergy until the French Revolution, which proved as fatal to the Scots College as to many similar institutions.

On 5 June 1790, Lord Robert Fitzgerald, the British Chargé d'Affaires, addressed a note to the French Government demanding protection for the Irish and Scots Colleges in Paris. A report issued a few months later stated that the British religious establishments in France numbered twenty-eight, with an estimated revenue of 329,000 livres.

By means of repeated appeals to the English Catholics, Bishop Hay succeeded in obtaining a substantial sum towards the relief of his impoverished mission and in the last year of the eighteenth century, he moved the seminary from Scalan – where it had existed for more than seventy-five years – to a larger and more convenient site at Aquhorties in Aberdeenshire.

These earlier years of Bishop Hay's vicariate were distinguished by the suppression of the Society of Jesus by Clement XIV. The Jesuit Fathers ceased to direct the Scots College in Rome, which was placed under a commission of five Cardinals. Notice of this change was given to Bishop Grant by Cardinal Castelli in August of 1773 with the proviso that he would also receive from the Nuncio at Brussels a copy of the brief of suppression. The twelve Jesuits ministering in Scotland expressed their willingness to comply with the orders of the Holy See.

Soon afterwards a dispute developed between the Vicars-apostolic and the Scots ex-Jesuits over the administration of the property once belonging to the Society. In a letter to Cardinal Castelli in June 1774, Bishop Hay requested that all this property, previously overseen by the Jesuits, should now be placed under the care of the bishops.

The rising of Charles Edward Stuart had greatly diminished the number of Catholics in Scotland. The General Assembly of 1779 estimated that the total number of Catholics was less than 20,000. Of this number no more than twenty possessed land, while in the business world there were none of any prominence.

These figures were somewhat at variance with the statistics sent by Bishop Hay to Rome, placing the number of communicants in the Scottish Mission at around 17,000. This raised the total number of Catholics to some 30,000.

As a guide to the position of Scottish Catholics in the late eighteenth century, it is worth reading the legal enactments summarised in the Statute Law abridged by Lord Kames:

> 'All professors of the Catholic religion were obliged to quit the country, unless they would subscribe the Confession of Faith. The purchase or dissemination of Catholic books was punishable with banishment and confiscation of personal property.
>
> Jesuits and seminary priests were to be pursued, apprehended and punished with death.
>
> Those guilty of hearing Mass, of refusing to attend the Protestant service, or of endeavouring to pervert any of his Majesty's subjects, either by reasoning or by books, were liable to the same penalty.'

It would be a long and lonely road toward a new enlightenment.

SCALAN

THE DARKEST PERIOD of the Catholic Church's history in Scotland often provides the most illuminating tales of bravery and loyalty in the face of persecution.

In 1701 all priests were banned from Scotland and outwith the Highland regions the Catholic population was almost non-existent. This was the backdrop to the origins of Scalan, a hidden seminary which was to ensure that the Catholic religion not only survived but eventually prospered.

Following the failed Jacobite rising in 1715, the British Government, supported by the Presbyterian Church, redoubled its efforts to eradicate what remained of the Catholic Church. Priests were seen as the most ardent supporters of the Jacobite cause and every effort was made to hunt them down and drive them into exile. Priests returning to Scotland had been in the Scots colleges in Madrid, Paris, Rome and Douai. But many were ill-prepared for life as an illegal missionary in Scotland. It was for this reason that the Scottish bishops sought a domestic training ground, which would allow them control over the selection process for candidates and in turn give the seminarians experience of the conditions in which they would serve.

The Braes of Glenlivet, in the north east, had been chosen as the site for this seminary, in part for their remoteness. But they also lay at the heart of an area populated by the last vestiges of Scotland's Catholic population. Glenlivet was a Highland property of the Dukes of Gordon, who remained Catholic. Unlike the Lowlanders, the Highland people had clung fiercely to their faith and in 1677 a Fr Alexander Leslie, reporting to the Vatican, said that 'in spite of their natural ferocity (the Highlanders) were as lambs in the presence of a priest, and as firm in their Faith as rocks.' There may have been no Catholics in Glasgow at that time, but there were more than one thousand in Lowland and Highland Banffshire. Nestled in this sanctuary and shielded by the barren Ladder Hills the seminary of Scalan was established in 1716. Opened by Bishop James Gordon, its aim was to provide the Catholic people with new priests of their own blood.

In his book, *Scalan: The Forbidden College*, Dr John Watts paints a picture of four young

Scalan college

Scalan college

attacks by the Government Redcoat soldiers. The attacks were urged on by local Presbyterian ministers who sought to close Scalan's doors. However, the local people of all faiths did not share their views. Local magistrates were inclined not to enforce the penal laws and the people of Glenlivet acted as look-outs warning the college and its staff of incoming Redcoats.

In one case a Fr Kilian Grant was taken prisoner but on appearing in court the magistrate and Laird of Ballindalloch, who was also a Grant, refused to convict him on the grounds that there was no evidence (except for the word of Fr Grant) that he was a priest – as 'papists' were incapable of telling the truth.

In the wake of the battle of Culloden soldiers were sent 'to extinguish the remains of the rebellion.' Look-outs warned the then rector, William Duthie, of their coming and he hid his students and the vestments and vessels. He then watched from a nearby hill as his beloved seminary was burned to the ground. During the following summer Duthie remained close by and built a new house, smaller than the first.

The first two men to receive their full training in Glenlivet were the 'Heather Priests' Hugh MacDonald latterly Bishop MacDonald and George Gordon. But the most celebrated figure in Scalan's history is Bishop George Hay. As a 16-year-old medical student he tended wounded Jacobites. In the wake of defeat he was imprisoned, where he then converted to Catholicism and later served at sea as a ship's surgeon. He was ordained to the priesthood at the Scots College in Rome and was consecrated bishop in the small upstairs chapel in Scalan on Trinity Sunday, 1769. He later consecrated Alexander MacDonald, Bishop and Vicar- apostolic of the Highland region in the same room on Passion Sunday in 1780. Bishop Hay lived at

boys, guided by one young priest, arriving at a small hut by the Crombie burn at the heart of the Braes. They came from the last bastions of the Catholic faith in the North East of Scotland and the Western Highlands and the life that they chose to follow was spartan in the extreme.

Their day began at six a.m., when they would rise and wash in the waters of the Crombie. They ate meals mainly consisting of oatmeal porridge and they had meat two or three times a week. Their curriculum later included Latin, Greek, Hebrew, geography, chronology, rhetoric and theology and they would study, pray, eat and sleep together in one small room.

The college was known to have twelve students at one point, but the usual figure was around five. Its primary function was to provide a launching point for the boys to go on to study on the continent, although some notable students received their full training there.

The 1720s were tumultuous for the seminary as it survived

The ruin of the north wing

In the years after the move to Aquhorties, the north wing of the seminary became a public church for the people of the braes. It later fell into disrepair but has recently been stablised.

Today the visitors book inside the College shows entries from all over Europe, America and beyond. This would surely have brought a smile to the face of Bishop Geddes, former college rector, who in 1777 wrote:

'The time by the Goodness of God will come when the Catholic religion will again flourish in Scotland; and then, when posterity shall acquire, with a laudable curiosity, by what means any sparks of the true faith were preserved in those dismal times of darkness and error, Scalan will be mentioned with veneration, and all that can be known about it will be recorded with care.'

Scalan for some years as rector and oversaw the building of a new college. He also lived to see more peaceful times and the beginnings of a new dawn for the Catholic Church.

Pressure on the Church eased during the French Wars. Bishop Hay made a hard decision. These were safer times, Scalan was too remote and a new and more accessible seminary was needed. He purchased a larger building in Aquhorties near Inverurie and in 1799 the boys came down from the mountains, concluding a vital chapter in the story of Scotland's Catholic Church.

Scalan's contribution to the well-being of Catholicism in Scotland is immeasurable. Without the 'Heather Priests' what would have happened to the thousands of Irish immigrants arriving in the West? The numbers of the faithful may have been bolstered by their arrival, but who would have ministered to their spiritual needs as they arrived here starving and impoverished?

Scalan College with the north wing in the foreground

The room where the boys ate and slept

Hidden seminary

Between 1716 and 1799, at a time when the Catholic Church was outlawed by Government decree, the college produced around one hundred priests.

Every year, on the first Sunday of July, people travel from throughout the country to take part in a Mass to honour the past and pray for the future and celebrate the heritage and legacy of Scalan, Scotland's hidden seminary. Getting to Scalan is no mean feat. Tucked away in the Braes of Glenlivet it is a half mile from the end of the public road. Today the empty seminary stands as a monument to the bravery and piety of the priests and people who kept the Catholic faith alive in the darkest of times.

Since its closure in 1799 Scalan has been used as a barn and a dwelling, but over the years fell into disrepair. It was the site of pilgrimage for artist Peter Anson in 1934. Shocked by the state of the building, he contacted the Bishops' Conference. In post war years, the Scalan Association was established by Canons MacWilliam and Bonnyman and Fr McRoberts. Together the group pledged to keep Scalan alive in the modern Church and through their endeavours the building was saved and its legacy preserved. By documenting Scalan's history the Association has succeeded in inspiring writings and a new wave of interest in the hidden seminary. In recent years under the leadership of Mgr John Copland, who was born in Glenlivet, the Scalan Association has attracted many new members and the building has been attractively restored.

Bishop's room inside the college

FANNING THE FLAMES

THE CRUSADE OF BISHOP HAY on behalf of Catholicism was an exercise in hope over expectation. In the late eighteenth century all professors of the Catholic religion were obliged to leave Scotland unless they subscribed to the Confession of Faith. The purchase or holding of Catholic books was punishable with confiscation of belongings and even banishment. Jesuits and seminary priests in particular were strongly pursued, apprehended and punished. Catholic books were to be destroyed and their importers committed to prison.

The Bishop had to contend with the command for presbyteries to 'summon all Papists, and those suspected of Papistry' and require them to renounce their faith before the Kirk. Failure to do this would incur further wrath. They would be brought before the Privy Council and any property they owned would be confiscated. The list of punishable 'offences' was endless.

Anyone suspected of being a priest, Jesuit, or 'trafficking Papist' and charged with changing his surname faced deportation with the certainty of death if he attempted to return. A similar penalty awaited any subject who attended a meeting 'where there is altar, Mass-book, vestments, Popish images, or other Popish trinkets'.

Draconian fines were imposed on parents from the nobility who sent their sons to be taught in seminaries overseas, while children under the care of Catholic parents and guardians were to be wrested from them and entrusted to a 'well-affected and religious friend' the finance for their education and support being provided from the property of their parents.

It was considered a serious crime to convert to Catholicism any of his Majesty's Protestant subjects, and by a convoluted procedure, Catholics were prevented from acquiring property, either by purchase, gifts, or in trust on their behalf. Such deeds were simply dismissed in law as null and void.

Similarly they were also denied after the age of fifteen the right to inherit estates. If the heir refused to renounce his faith, the right of succession lapsed, passing to the nearest Protestant heir. If the latter refused to accept the estate it passed to the next Protestant after him, and so on until the right was 'effectually established' in the Protestant line.

A Protestant turning Catholic effectively became a non-person. In the way that Negroes in the Southern states of America were disenfranchised and native South Africans were subject to discriminatory laws the Catholic minority were subjugated by a ruthless and unrelenting oppressor. It is difficult to envisage the extent of this discrimination and yet it remains much more than a distant memory. All donations and legacies in favour of 'cloisters or other Popish societies' were by that fact null and void.

In the *History of the Catholic Church of Scotland*, Alphons Bellesheim writes:

> 'By the operation of these iniquitous statutes, the adherents of the ancient faith in Scotland had been gradually reduced to a condition little better than that of slaves and outlaws.
>
> The amelioration of this state of affairs was an object well fitted to enlist the mental vigour and wide sympathies of Bishop Hay and the fact that a Relief Bill in favour of the English Catholics was at the time passing through Parliament, served to encourage him in his efforts.'

The tide of public opinion was turning toward an encouraging era of tolerance. An ironic twist of events which were intended to prevent such concessions to Catholics, actually helped to move forward Catholic emancipation.

An agitation sprang up in Scotland against moves to provide even the minimum of relief from the penal laws. It descended into a wild outburst of fanaticism, fanning the flames of dissent when Lord George Gordon seized upon the rumour that the Government was considering some relaxation in the penal laws to arouse a storm of Protestant opposition.

The General Assembly had stated in 1778 that 'disastrous consequences' would result from any measure of Catholic relief. In October, a few months after the meeting of the Assembly, the Synod of Glasgow and Ayr appointed a general fast day in the cities to counteract the 'awful signs of divine displeasure which are visibly displayed at this time, particularly the encouragement given to and the growth of Popery'. Not surprisingly, the spark having been lit, there were the inevitable bonfires.

The Sunday following the meeting of the Synod a frenzied mob surrounded a private house in Glasgow, where a Catholic service was being celebrated. The people emerging from the house were jeered and pelted with stones and dirt. The mob broke all the windows, ripped the doors off their hinges, and robbed the home of its contents.

In the words of one eyewitness, the rabble was 'breathing blood and slaughter, to all Papists, and in every respect profaned the Lord's Day in a grosser manner than I ever knew done in Britain'.

Thus in that year Glasgow's Catholics were deprived of their only chapel.

Outside the church

ST MARY'S in FOCHABERS

ST MARY'S CHURCH IN FOCHABERS is at the core of the lands once ruled by the Gordons, the protectors of the Catholic faith during the Reformation and penal times which followed. Risking their titles, lands and lives the Gordons harboured outlaw missionaries in their properties and helped support the Catholic Church and Jacobite Rebellions over a period of two hundred years.

Successive dukes reinforced the position of the Church, defending the Catholic faithful from persecution and donating money for the training and support of priests.

It was on Gordon land that the Scottish Mission established the hidden national seminary at Scalan and it was with the Gordons' blessing that priests ministered to the spiritual needs of the local Catholic population.

The family also rallied to the Jacobite cause in 1715, although in 1745 it took a more cautious approach. The then Duke, Cosmo George, distanced himself from the rising and two of his brothers even served in the Government army. At Gordon Castle, however a third brother, Lewis, was recruiting men for the Jacobites while allowing the family home to be used as a rebel headquarters. At least two local priests, Fr Kilian Grant and Fr John Tyrie, served this Gordon-led Jacobite division as chaplains.

Near Gordon Castle lay an ancient chapel, thought to have been founded in 1362, which was maintained and funded by the family. A further three Catholic places of worship sheltered beneath the shadow of the castle. Catholic worship continued in Bog of Gight up until the death of the Duke in 1728. Following his death the family, led by the dowager Duchess, converted to Protestantism. In spite of this she continued, like many local people of the Protestant tradition, to be sympathetic to the Catholic Church and to support and shield the Scalan seminary, meeting regularly with the bishops and priests.

In 1826, three years before Catholic emancipation, the current St Mary's church opened in Fochabers. The foundation stone of the Gothic Church had been laid the year before and its beauty matched that of the other new church projects in the area. Today all that

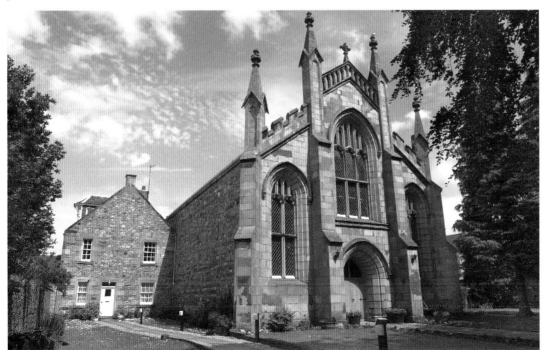

The gothic facade of St Mary's church in Fochabers

The beautifully peaceful interior of St Mary's in Fochabers

beauty remains. The Gothic façade masks a stunning interior in which light hues are highlighted by the natural light from the stained glass windows. Few structural changes were made until the Second Vatican Council, although the care lavished on the church by successive communities has succeeded in maintaining this gem in the north east.

The stained glass windows of St Mary's in Fochabers

ST THOMAS'S

THE OPENING OF ST THOMAS'S CHURCH in Keith in 1831 further marked the resurgence of the Catholic faith in Scotland. As the persecution of Catholicism faded and an air of tolerance swept through society, the Scottish Mission activated dormant plans for a programme of widespread church building. In 1825 a Fr Walter Lovi began planning for a church to serve the local Catholic population in Keith. Long recognised as one of the country's Catholic strongholds, Keith's faithful had previously gathered for Mass in a small chapel on the outskirts of town.

When planning the new place of worship Fr Lovi travelled through England, France and Ireland, studying examples of these countries' finest architectural achievements. He was also determined to construct the new church in a prime location within the town.

A native of Edinburgh, Fr Lovi had gained a number of friends in high places, one of whom was Charles X, the King of France. While visiting Paris, Fr Lovi contacted the King with a request for a contribution toward the building of the new church in Scotland. A donation soon followed, as well as the promise of a painting of *The Incredulity of St Thomas* by the artist Francois Dubois, which would give the church an altar piece. Returning to Keith news reached Fr Lovi of the 1830 Revolution in France and the exile of his friend Charles. The treasured painting had gone missing during his flight and was given up as lost but Fr Lovi, not to be put off, returned to France, tracking down the painting to the Louvre Gallery and returning with it to Keith in time for the opening of the new church.

Today the painting still carries the Royal seal of Charles X on the back and bears a brass plate on the front naming Charles as the benefactor.

The new church was opened on 7 August 1831 by Bishop James Kyle, but it would be a further eighty-five years before St Thomas's took on its present form. Externally the most striking feature of the building is the domed roof which rises from the back of the church. Designed by the architect Charles Menart, the copper dome was completed in 1916 along with a number of internal adjustments, including a new niche for Dubois' painting and a new altar. Perhaps the most remarkable part of

The church of St Thomas in Keith

Statues outside the church of St Thomas

this chapter in St Thomas's history is that the parishioners raised more than sixty per cent of the £3000 needed for the work, a very large amount at the time.

Today the church stands as a symbol of the long and often turbulent history of the Catholic faith in the area.

JOHN OGILVIE

The ancient parish of Keith is also the birthplace of one of Scotland's most famous saints, John Ogilvie.

Born in 1579 in nearby Drum, John was the eldest son of the Scots noble Walter Ogilvie and was raised as a Calvinist. At thirteen he left home to study on the continent. Five years later he entered the Scots College in Douai and declared that he wished to convert to the Catholic faith. In the next two years his studies took him to the Benedictine College and then to the Jesuits in Ratisbon. By 1599 he was a novice of the Jesuit Order in Brunn. From the date of his ordination in 1610 Fr Ogilvie repeatedly asked to be sent back to his homeland to serve the Scottish Mission, though he knew well the dangers of this work.

At this time the persecution of Catholics was at a peak, with priests and active laity being hunted by Government soldiers. Those captured were tortured for the names of fellow Catholics and were either executed or banished for their crimes.

In November 1613, the young priest's request was finally granted and at the age of thirty-four Fr John Ogilvie returned to Scotland to serve the Lowlands as a missionary. While travelling he posed as a horse dealer and at times as a soldier named Watson, serving an area which included Glasgow, Edinburgh and Renfrewshire.

His life as a missionary was to last just one year. In order to best serve the area's fractured Catholic community the priest had to entrust his life to the faithful, with betrayal meaning imprisonment and possible death. While in Glasgow he was contacted by an Adam Boyd, the nephew of the local sheriff, who begged Fr Ogilvie to instuct him in the Catholic Faith. At their meeting place Fr Ogilvie was arrested by Government soldiers and imprisoned. He was questioned by the Protestant Archbishop Spottiswoode of Glasgow using questions sent by King James VI himself. Despite enduring tortures, which included being deprived of sleep for eight days and nine nights, Fr Ogilvie did not reveal any names.

Although he declared his loyalty to King James, he would not attest to the King's supremacy over the Pope in spiritual matters. He was even offered his freedom along with the provostship of Moffat and the hand of the archbishop's daughter in marriage, if he would renounce the Pope. His patience, courage and even humour during his imprisonment won the admiration of his captors.

However this admiration could not save Fr Ogilvie and on 10 March 1615 he was led to the scaffold at Glasgow Cross and hanged before the crowd. His final words were: 'If there be here any hidden Catholics, let them pray for me but the prayers of heretics I will not have.' His body was spared the insult of being drawn and quartered, perhaps due to public sympathy and he was hurriedly buried in the churchyard of Glasgow Cathedral.

He was declared Venerable in the seventeenth century, beatified by Pope Pius XI in 1929 and canonised St John Ogilvie in 1976. He is Scotland's only officially recognised martyr.

RESPITE FROM PERSECUTION

O N BISHOP HAY'S RETURN to Scotland in 1782 he discovered that for the Church to survive there had to be the barest contribution of financial support. During his stay in London, he had consulted with figures of authority with a view to their lobbying the Government for a relaxation of the penal laws. He also aimed to secure money for the Catholic clergy. This would be achieved by the announcement that an annual grant would now be made available to the Church for its labours. It greatly assisted in widening the mission and undoubtedly helped the conversions to Catholicism which were taking place.

Further developments such as the benevolent interest of the Duke of Gordon in the large number of Catholic tenants on his estates helped to encourage the mission of the bishops and their people.

The last decade of the eighteenth century saw the death of two of Scotland's bishops. The vicar-apostolic of the Highlands, Alexander MacDonald died on 9 September 1791. His successor John Chisholm was consecrated the following year by Bishop Hay and in 1799 Bishop Geddes died at Aberdeen. Pius VI nominated Alexander Cameron as coadjutor to Bishop Hay in 1797 in place of the ailing John Geddes.

At the beginning of a new century, the Church hierarchy was taking stock of a rapidly changing landscape. It was becoming clear that the penal laws had been ineffectual in destroying the allegiance of the remaining Catholics to their faith. The gradual progress of democratic enlightenment was making discrimination indefensible.

In 1800 Scotland had 2 bishops, 40 priests, 12 churches and 30,000 adherents. However, it was a foreign preoccupation which was to produce a beneficial climate for the faith.

The power of Napoleon reduced internal politics in Britain to minor importance and it made sense for the Establishment to unite all citizens against an outside enemy. Napoleon calculated that by landing in Ireland he could exploit the long-term hostility between the Irish and the English. The Government struggled to remove the possible sparking of religious and political dissent. Scarcely credible was the fact that exiled Catholic clergy from France were welcomed by the British state and general public alike.

Bishop Horsley of the Anglican Church said:

> 'No one has a better claim to this proof of our affection than these men, from whose doctrines and observances we are so widely sundered. These estimable prelates and clergy of the fallen Church of France have won a place in our hearts by the edifying example which they have given of patience under the sufferings which they are now enduring for conscience sake.'

Bishop Hay had discussed with French bishops the possibility of several of their emigrant clergy coming to assist in the Scottish Mission. Soon afterwards six French priests were labouring for the faith in the Lowlands of the country.

Taking their lead from England, the Protestants of Scotland offered the Catholic Church a short-term respite from persecution. During this time it was possible for Church leaders to make progress in clawing back some of their organisation and power.

It was with relief and hope for the future that in 1804 Bishop Hay announced that the persecution of Catholics was ended. There were twenty-eight missionaries in the Lowlands under the control of their bishop and receiving ten pounds annually from the common fund. There were no regular clergy and no convent of nuns in the country. The Catholic population did not join in communion with their Protestant neighbours and would not enter their churches. Catholics did frequently enter into marriage with Protestant partners – always before a Catholic priest. This was how the Catholic Church saw itself in the Scotland of the early 1800s.

Perhaps it is even more instructive to read the perceptions of non-Catholics. In 1810 Thomas Chalmers wrote:

> 'There still continues in Scotland the remains of the most ancient Church, after all the efforts of reformation, all the harshness of severity and all the influences of kindness; so difficult is it to eradicate the religious habits of a people. These Roman Catholics are generally poor and helpless, quiet and inoffensive, which are qualities that anywhere merit and receive the protection of wise governments.'

ST NINIAN'S CEMETERY

THE MORAY CHURCH TRAIL has a habit of hiding its treasures in the most unlikely of places. Chapels in barns, Mass sites in forests and now the area's most ancient place of worship hidden amid the Banffshire farmlands. St Ninian's Cemetery in Enzie must be one of the region's most beautiful and peaceful sites.

Off the main road, across a farm road and through two iron gates, St Ninian's Cemetery is the resting place of two dozen of Scotland's Catholic priests. It is the oldest Catholic site in Enzie, first accommodating a Catholic church in around 1602 and again between 1687–88.

The priest of that time, John Irvine, built and cared for the parish and its people until the 1688 Revolution threw the nation into turmoil and saw the Catholic faith outlawed. As priests were driven underground or exiled, the churches were abandoned or taken over and John Irvine's church in the graveyard soon fell into disrepair. In later years Dr Alexander Geddes, the priest in the nearby hidden church of St Ninian's, stripped the roof of its slates for his own church. Today nothing is left of John Irvine's church except the keystone on the priest's mortuary chapel at the south of the graveyard. The Dawson Memorial Chapel, built by Robert Fairley, contains the mortal remains of two dozen priests, as well as a striking Crucifix, made by Hew Lorimer.

A granite cross nearby marks the grave of Scotland's first Catholic post-Reformation bishop, Thomas Nicolson. In 1677 the priest, Alexander Leslie, had reported to Rome that 'a general superior for Scotland with authority over both seculars and regulars' was urgently required. This was the first move to appoint a Vicar-apostolic for Scotland, although it was not until 16 March 1694 that a leader for Scotland's Catholics was appointed. Born in Birkenbog, Banffshire and raised an Episcopalian, Thomas Nicolson was a 'late starter' in the priesthood. Educated in Aberdeen and Glasgow his ordination at forty closed the door on what would have been a successful and profitable career as an academic. His chosen vocation also made him an outlaw and he was to become well-acquainted with prisons and places of exile during the next thirty-two years.

The Dawson Memorial Chapel and graveyard at St Ninian's Cemetery

During his enforced exile in France, between 1689-94, he was secretly consecrated as Vicar-apostolic for Scotland. This move helped save the Catholic faith in Scotland, giving leadership to a Church which had been driven underground.

Thomas Nicolson was described as 'a very great man, both in learning and piety, under whom the mission was always free from intestine embroils'. This is quite an achievement considering the severity of the situation, the poverty of the Mission and lack of priests and is one of the reasons that so many pilgrims are drawn to this remote graveyard in the north-eastern corner of the country.

The Dawson Memorial Chapel

The striking Crucifix made by Hew Lorimer

ST NINIAN'S in TYNET

EVEN TODAY NO-ONE WOULD GUESS by looking at St Ninian's in Tynet that it is a church. It may look old, but the building is like any other old farmhouse or steading and there are no signs or symbols to hint otherwise. However, this simple, low, whitewashed building is Scotland's oldest post-Reformation Catholic church and like Scalan and Preshome, a symbol of the perseverance of the Catholic people of Enzie.

St Ninian's in Tynet

The thought of celebrating Mass in the dead of night in an open field or farmyard barn, in all weathers and in all seasons, must seem to us bad enough but add to this the threat of raids by soldiers and the certainty of imprisonment and you have the reality of Catholic life in Scotland in post-Reformation times.

Any moves toward establishing a more permanent place of worship would have been too dangerous even to consider – unless that plan was hatched in Enzie. The Catholic population there enjoyed the protection of the Gordon family and had never allowed their faith to be injured by the anti-Catholic measures enforced by Kirk and Government. For over two centuries the Tynet area alone had produced no fewer than eleven bishops and a larger number of priests.

Having had their old chapel in St Ninian's graveyard taken from them in 1725, the local Catholic people gathered for Mass in a barn belonging to the Laird of Tynet. But in the wake of the rebellion of '45, the barn was gutted and torched by soldiers returning from Culloden. This happened to many places of worship in Scotland, but particular vehemence was reserved for Enzie, an area which volunteered around 1200 men for the Jacobite army, a number which included Catholic priests.

By 1755 much of the danger had subsided and the Laird of Tynet built a sheep cote between the Tulloch and Auchenhalrig areas for the supposed use of his workers and labourers. In reality the building was a secret and illegal Mass centre for the local Catholic population.

These were the simple beginnings of the church that stands there today. The priests who served the area travelled disguised as farmers and said Mass in the dead of night. Despite the dangers the Catholic population increased until by 1787 the building had to be extended.

The interior of St Ninian's in Tynet

Today the church carries many reminders of its past. Crowning the west gable is a ball of stone, a reminder of the days of persecution. Inside, a dove hangs from the ceiling, taken from the ruins of the old church which once stood in the nearby St Ninian's graveyard. In the early 1930s it was decided to build a new church and abandon the old barn. Ironically the Second World War saved St Ninian's, putting an end to plans for a new one.

It is the oldest Catholic post-Reformation church still used for regular worship and one of the most beautiful and simple jewels hidden on the Moray Church Trail.

ST PETER'S

THE TWIN GOTHIC SPIRES of St Peter's Church rise above the town of Buckie on the North Sea coast. The dominant landmark on the north east skyline, the spires are still an inspirational sight.

St Peter's was built following the Act of Catholic Emancipation of 1829 which sanctioned an extensive programme of church rebuilding. A new church for new times, its construction in 1857 was of particular importance to the sizeable Catholic community in Buckie for whom the nearest place of worship had previously been St Gregory's at Preshome. The opening of the twin towered building signalled the beginning of a new Catholic community.

St Peter's was built on a site given by the Gordons of Letterfourie, a Catholic family who had supported the Church for centuries. The two Gordon brothers, Sir James and Sir Robert are buried there.

Bishop James Kyle's place in history is also secured. Not only did he design St Peter's but it is primarily thanks to his efforts that the Catholic Church has such an extensive library today. In his time as bishop he collected around 70,000 books and documents relating to Catholic life and dating as far back as 1597.

The interior of St Peter's matches the exterior for beauty. Over the years it has become customary for the parish priest to modify the appearance of the church. Under the guidance of the present priest, Fr Eddie Traynor, a number of notable features have been added. The most stunning of these is the organ, formerly belonging to Fort Augustus Abbey, which is fitted at the back of the hall. Everywhere in the building there is evidence of paintings or personal touches added by local people.

Outside St Peter's

The painting of Jesus and the Apostles. The spires of St Peter's can be seen on the distant shoreline.

The magnificent organ in St Peter's

Inside St Peter's

A BISHOP'S PLEA

ON 9 FEBRUARY 1779 an attack on the Catholics of Glasgow was planned by an organisation called, 'Friends to Protestantism'.

Following the destruction of their chapel an Englishman who was living in the city put his own home at their disposal. Mr Bagnall, who had introduced Staffordshire pottery into Glasgow, watched his house and adjacent warehouses burn to the ground. The capital city had witnessed similar scenes a couple of days before.

Bishop Hay wrote to the Vatican on 12 February,

'the promise of the ministry and of other influential persons, that the same indulgence (i.e., a Relief Bill) should be extended to Scotland in the first session of Parliament.'

No sooner did this become publicly known than the fanatic party among the preachers commenced to excite the alarm of the people. Catholics could not appear without being pointed at, and saluted with cries: 'See the Papist, the black Papist! Shoot him, kill him!'

In March the fury of the Edinburgh mob erupted and a vicious attack was perpetrated against a newly erected chapel-house in Chalmers' Close.

'So thickly rained the stones from all quarters,' wrote Bishop Hay, 'that they (Revs Cameron and Mathison) could make no resistance and only escaped with the greatest difficulty.'

By early evening the rioters had forced entry to the chapel-house and with stones and hammers wrecked the insides, setting it on fire. Several houses belonging to Catholics were looted and destroyed which the Edinburgh authorities not only failed to prevent but, once under way, proved incapable of stopping.

In contrast to this wave of excitement there were individuals who stood firm against the tide of intolerance – even from within the Protestant populace. Among those who did so was the University's Principal Robertson, whose oration before the 1779 General Assembly stands out as upright against the onslaught which threatened to engulf the entire Catholic minority. He said:

'My character as a man, as a citizen and as a minister of the Gospel has been delineated in the most odious colours. I have been represented as a pensioner of the Pope, as an agent for Rome, as a seducer of my brethren to Popery and as the tool of a king and ministry bent on overturning the Protestant religion.'

It was perhaps such encouraging signs of instilling tolerance that spurred Bishop Hay on amid dispiriting conditions. He visited London and conveyed to King George III the loyal regards of his Catholic subjects. This was accepted by the monarch and led to the bishop's involvement in talks with Government Ministers over the Catholic Relief Bill's progress through Parliament. Lords Germain and Weymouth were publicly supportive of the Bill.

There existed a plan, given much credence by persecuted Catholics in Scotland at the time, for mass emigration to Spain. Lord Linton expressed his support for the proposition, and the Spanish ambassador, among others, pledged the co-operation of his Government. This project was eventually abandoned.

However, the immediate difficulties of remaining in Scotland were many. Church leaders, led by Bishop Hay, drew up a comprehensive account of the sufferings of Catholic people. It was circulated to the legislature and a petition was presented to the King, who referred it to the consideration of Parliament.

Catholics were asking for an end to discrimination and compensation for their losses and a guarantee that such abominations would never be repeated. They pledged their commitment and loyalty to their country and asked in return for the protection of the state in the practice of their faith.

There were early signs that the petition was making an impact among its intended audience. Before the petition was put before Parliament, the MP for Middlesex, Mr Wilkes, raised the issue before the House. He asked the question: 'On what ground the concessions granted to the English Catholics were still being refused to their Scottish co-religionists?' Clearly, the fight was joined even if it had not yet been won.

ST GREGORY'S

IT WAS UNDOUBTEDLY THE STRENGTH of Catholicism in Enzie which convinced Scotland's hierarchy that the time and location were right for the building of the first obviously Catholic church since the Reformation. The Gordon family had ensured that the area would be safe for Catholics and even for the training of priests in the hidden seminary of Scalan. In addition, the local Protestant people were, by and large, sympathetic to their neighbours' plight and consistently turned a 'blind eye' to their illegal activities. Until the building of the magnificient church of St Gregory in Preshome, the Catholic Mass had been served in the most unlikely of venues. Fields, hilltops, forests and churches disguised as barns had all provided adequate cover for the outlaw priests and the illegal gathering of the faithful.

St Gregory's, hidden in the countryside of the north-east, was to become the nerve centre of the Catholic Church in Scotland. In 1788, Fr John Reid, the priest in charge of the eastern half of Enzie, felt confident enough to propose the building of a church. Although the extent of persecution was diminishing, to openly build a Catholic place of worship would have provoked action from the Kirk.

St Gregory's Church

For this reason, Preshome was chosen as the perfect site. Away from major routes and the watchful eye of soldiers, work began, funded by the local Baron of Letterourie and his brother, of the Gordon clan. The foundation stone of the church was laid by the brothers on 29 May 1788. Work was completed in 1790 and the church was opened on 23 May of that year.

Designed by Fr Reid, St Gregory's shows much of the beauty of the buildings of Rome, where Fr Reid had studied, as well as a number of local influences. This blend is most evident in the façade of the building and the interior, where local Portsoy marble has been shaped for the holy water stoups.

Since it was first built changes have been made. The sanctuary has been enlarged at the expense of the old sacristy and in 1990 an extensive refurbishment was completed at a cost of £100,000. In part the money came from the Historic Buildings Council while the fifteen parishioners of the church have struggled to raise the deficit.

The interior of St Gregory's

Preshome was also chosen for its importance to the national Church. In 1697 Scotland's first bishop since the Reformation, Thomas Nicolson, moved to the area, making it the headquarters of the Catholic Church in Scotland for two centuries. This era ended with the passing of Bishop James Kyle in 1869.

Bishop Kyle is credited with preserving, compiling and recovering archives detailing centuries of Catholic life in Scotland. This collection, containing in excess of 30,000 items, was transferred to the Blairs College Library and then given on long-term loan to the National Library of Scotland in 1974.

Today, St Gregory's maintains all its former beauty and is a lasting symbol of the bravery of the early Catholic communities of Scotland.

St Gregory's façade

Archives of Catholic life in Scotland

AT THE MERCY OF THE MOB

ON 18 MARCH 1779, a petition signed by Scotland's Catholics was brought before Parliament. The progressive philosopher, Edmund Burke, stood on the side of the petitioners. He read before Parliament the contents of a small pamphlet. It contained examples of penal laws relating to Scottish Catholics and he challenged any member to endorse this catalogue of discrimination.

None did so, but the motion to consider the controversial petition fell, due to the absence of support from the Government. It was clearly too far a step to contemplate.

The year 1780 saw a further reawakening of fervour when the Protestant Association gathered in London. The president, Lord George Gordon, read out a brief addressed by the Pope to the Catholics of England. It called for his people to lobby Parliament and seek no less than the repeal of the penal laws.

In June of that year more than 20,000 people marched to the Houses of Parliament, carrying with them a petition claiming to contain 120,000 signatures.

There were violent outbursts against members of both Houses and the chapels of the Sardinian and Bavarian embassies were set on fire. For more than three days the city was at the mercy of an uncontrollable mob. When calm was restored a royal proclamation described the demolition of the embassy chapels as a violation of international right.

An eyewitness to the rioting wrote:

'The month of June 1780 will ever be marked by a dark and diabolical fanaticism which I supposed to be extinct, but which actually subsists in Great Britain perhaps beyond any other country in Europe.'

The outbursts had their desired effect. It took twelve years for Scottish Catholics to be freed from the repression of the penal laws.

In April of 1793 the Lord Advocate was granted permission to initiate a long-awaited measure of relief. A Bill securing freedom for Catholics from all pains and penalties enforced by former Acts was passed into law. It also allowed them the possession and free disposition of their property.

The drawback was that they continued to be excluded from virtually every public office. This included that of professor and teacher, and they were still compelled to be married by the parish minister, to pay dues for baptism to the parish officials and a Protestant consenting to be married by a priest would be heavily fined and censured by the Kirk.

On 8 July 1793, the three Scottish bishops wrote to Pope Pius VI expressing their satisfaction at the developments. Bishop Hay showed his gratitude towards the Government by publishing a pastoral letter voicing his loyalty to the state and calling for the public prayers to be offered up for the king. Despite this, Bishop Hay remained zealous in his campaign to extend emancipation.

In 1779, the Bishop of Tiberiopolis and Vicar-apostolic of the Highlands, John MacDonald, died and Alexander MacDonald was nominated as his successor. Several months passed before John Geddes, rector of the seminary in Spain, was named by the Holy See as coadjutor to Bishop Hay in the Lowland district.

Among the crucial matters which required the attention of the bishops was the position of the two national colleges at Paris and Rome. For many years they had need of further renovation and a strengthening of spiritual support.

To assist these moves, Bishop Hay made a trip to Rome in 1781, travelling by way of Belgium, resting at Spa, where he met the Papal Nuncio and the Princess of Stolberg, mother-in-law of Charles Edward Stuart.

Reaching Rome, he had mixed news to impart: after the Jacobite rising of 1745, the subscription of the clergy was required to the orthodoxy imposed under Pope Alexander VII and extended by Clement XII in 1736. It had subsequently fallen into disuse. He pointed out the need for a new ritual for Scotland and an increase in the yearly grant made to the Scottish mission.

His proposals met with success and a ritual which he drew up was soon printed and officially sanctioned by the Vatican. Unfortunately, one of the principal projects of the bishop was not put into operation.

After the suppression of the Society of Jesus, Cardinal Marefoschi, the guardian of the Scots College in Rome, had asked the Scottish bishops to select a fit candidate for the role of rector from among their own clergy. The bishops had refused to comply with this plea. An Italian priest was once again appointed and despite the best efforts of subsequent Vicars-apostolic, who regretted the refusal, the college continued to be governed by Italian superiors for almost forty years.

Bishop Hay wrote to Pope Pius VI in 1782 expressing his disappointment at the circumstances surrounding the Scots College. It was too late. The Catholic hierarchy in Scotland was to take many generations to reach the required level of self-confidence.

OUR LADY AND ST BEAN

THE CHAPEL AND PRESBYTERY of Our Lady and St Bean in Marydale is situated in the village of Cannich, in the glen of Strathglass. The building dates from 1868 and is a testament to a region which has played an important role in the history of Catholicism in Scotland. Its roots go back to the time of St Bean in the late sixth century and the church is dedicated to him.

Even as the Reformation swept through the country the people of Cannich remained Catholic and the region was to play a key role in the revival of the Catholic faith in the Highlands in the eighteenth century.

A new crisis now faces the little church and the adjoining buildings which face collapse as damp and rot eat the structures.

The church of Marydale stands at the entrance to the glen and tradition states that the Gospel was first preached in the area by St Bean, a cousin of St Columba, who became the second abbot of Iona after Columba died.

As the Reformation took hold, the laird, a member of the Chisholm family, was imprisoned in 1579 for retaining his Catholic faith. Later Strathglass lairds adhered to the state religion but the populace of Glen Cannich remained stoutly Catholic.

Despite a climate of sanctions it was on Strathglass that the Jesuit mission of 1580–1600 focussed its attention and triggered the revival of Catholicism in the late seventeenth century. This culminated in the building of the church of Marydale.

The church requires a good deal of restoration. A former member of the Fort Augustus community reports:

'The building is important from a historical, architectural and local community point of view. It was opened in 1868 and is the last in a succession of mission churches in the area which began during the continued Catholic revival of the late eighteenth century.

The church was designed by the well-known church architect Joseph Hansom and is regarded as one of the best examples of his work. It would be a tragedy if it was allowed to rot and crumble. The church and presbytery

The Chapel and Presbytery

Font from old church of 1801

The old baptismal font

Triggered by the conversion of Colin Chisholm of Knockfin to Catholicism a series of churches were built. Two small chapels at Knockfin and Clachan Comar were opened in 1801 but they were later replaced by grander churches, including Our Lady and St Bean. The larger churches, such as Marydale, are linked with the smaller through original items like the holy water font at Our Lady and St Bean, which dates back to a Jesuit priest, Fr John Farquharson, who was known locally as 'Maghistair Ian'.

are still in use and serve an area as far afield as Drumnadrochit thirteen miles to the east. There are two services each week which are attended all the year by the local parishioners and by visitors during the summer months.'

It is a beautiful church with the chapel and presbytery forming an L-shape and the adjacent buildings set in a small courtyard. The buildings form part of the Sancti Angeli Benedictine Skete which is open as a retreat for those wanting to try monastic life. Marydale offers the ideal location for the monastic life with its air of silence and tranquillity.

The chapel contains a small stone-roofed bell tower leading to a choir balcony overlooking the chapel and the polished marble altar.

Visiting the glen in the eighteenth century, he took to wearing the kilt like the local men and made a collection of Gaelic Poetry. He was twice taken prisoner and in between times resided under a large boulder at the Brae of Craskie in the glen. Inside his hideaway he used the 'Clach-a-Bhaistidh' – a hollowed out stone or cupstone – as a baptismal font. This cupstone is on a pillar outside the church at Marydale.

The Catholic revival continued and the Chisholm brothers, John and Aeneas continued the Strathglass mission. In 1792 John was consecrated Bishop of the Highland region and in 1814 his brother

The interior of church

succeeded him. While serving as bishop Aeneas built a church at Fasnakyle to replace the smaller one at Clachan Comar. By 1868 the larger church at Marydale was opened and the baptismal font was placed at the church entrance.

If the church building was to fall further into disrepair it would not only be detrimental to the image of the picturesque village but it could signify the end of centuries of struggle to built the church here in the first place.

A STEP IN THE RIGHT DIRECTION

THE LAST REFERENCE TO BISHOP HAY stated that from his retirement in 1805 he lived in the seminary of Aquhorties. He died in October 1811 at the age of 83.

At that time the Lowland and Highland districts were governed by two bishops. Large numbers of Catholic Highlanders uprooted themselves and their families, moving to the industrial cities of the south and many even to Canada.

In 1802 Highland emigrants sailed for the New World under the guidance of Fr Alexander Macdonald who was later to become the first Bishop of Kingston in Upper Canada.

Bishop John Chisholm died in 1814 and was succeeded in the Highland vicariate by his brother, Aeneas. His death in 1818 led to the appointment of Fr Ranald MacDonald, who was consecrated at Edinburgh in February 1820.

The first quarter of the 1800s witnessed the slow but sure development of Catholicism throughout Scotland. Between 1800–1829 churches were established in Aberdeen, Dumfries, Edinburgh, Greenock, and Dundee, among others. This resulted in the revival of Catholicism in several of its former strongholds, while the substantial influx of Irish immigrants aided the increase. In Edinburgh and Leith, the number of Catholics increased from 1000 in 1800 to 14,000 in 1829 and in Dundee that same year they reached 1500. In Aberdeen they stood at 3000. Demand was outstripping supply, as chapels were failing to cater for the numbers who wished to worship.

The original Blairs College, with the chapel overlooking the walled garden. To the left is the extension built in the 1850s. On the extreme left can be seen the spire of the present church.

In 1821 Glasgow's priest, Andrew Scott, raised the profile of the Church by suing for slander the publication, *The Protestant*. He had incurred the wrath of the publication by building a beautiful church despite numerous obstacles. Patience wore thin when the publication accused him of extorting money from 'the sweat and sinews and blood' of his distressed flock, under threat of eternal damnation in the next world. Damages of £2000 were awarded to Fr Scott. It was little more than a symbolic victory, but it was a strong and important indication of change nonetheless.

Andrew Scott was later to become the second Vicar-apostolic of the Western District and his efforts to promote Catholicism in Glasgow were to prove fruitful. By 1829 the Catholic population in the city had increased to 25,000 and Scotland-wide stood at 70,000. As a consequence of this upsurge Pope Leo XII created a new partition of the Scottish mission, dividing it into three vicariates, namely the Eastern, Western, and Northern.

There still remained hostility from the Presbyterian majority and it took the Government of 1829 to repeal the remaining laws discriminating against Catholics.

This, in itself, was met by strong opposition from the English Tories, who had lobbied for the enactment of these same laws during the reign of William III.

The political rise of O'Connell to power in Ireland assisted the reforms, which in turn provoked descendants of the Covenanters to set up anti-Catholic demonstrations throughout Scotland. Villages and towns were soon exhibiting scenes of protest unseen since the days of James VI.

A petition circulated in the capital against the emancipation of Catholics garnered 18,000 signatures and one in Glasgow achieved double this figure.

Parliament pressed on regardless and in April of 1829, the Act received its royal assent. Undoubtedly a step in the right direction but the legislation was not a panacea for all ills of the Catholics.

The prohibition of Jesuits and monastic orders remained in force as did the refusal of State support for Catholic schools in Scotland. For years afterwards no Catholic priest could hold a position as chaplain in a workhouse, prison or hospital.

Keen to capitalise on these concessions, the Vicars-apostolic met and issued new regulations governing Church property, appointing professors and disciplines to be observed by students. One omission in the spiritual landscape was the absence of a single convent of nuns. This was rectified in 1832 when Fr Gillis wrote to inform Pope Gregory XVI that an Ursuline convent in Edinburgh had been founded. This was greeted with great enthusiasm among the Catholic populace and even many Protestants afforded them and their works a welcome. More widespread support was aroused by the devotion shown by the nuns during a traumatic outbreak of cholera in that same year. This recognition of the selfless acts of the Catholic community did much to elevate the Church in the eyes of the Protestant public.

Clearly laws might not change attitudes but the Catholic Church, leading by example, could pave the way towards understanding and respect.

ST COLUMBA (COLUM CILLE)

THE SMALL ISLAND OF IONA plays a significant part in the story of Scotland's Christian heritage. After Columba had arrived and founded his abbey the island formed a vital link between Church communities in Ireland and the rest of the monastic world. Despite the turmoil of the Churches in the seventh century the community of Iona had grown to 150 and the cult of Columba had spread far and wide across Scotland. Much of the credit goes to Adamnan, the ninth abbot of Iona who was a visitor to the Pictish lands.

Indeed, the Picts left as many dedications to Adamnan as they did to Columba, which is a testament to his influence in spreading the cult of Colum Cille. Adamnan's work did not end with the Picts for there is evidence that he was respected in Ireland, Dalriada, Strathclyde and in Northumberland. It was during his time that the power of the Ionan church reached its height. Around 697, Adamnan put forward his Law of the Innocents giving protection to children, women, and religion during times of war. This was widely accepted by kings and commoners.

Iona was soon to lose its status. The great plague in Ireland of 664 weakened the community and Viking raids at the turn of the ninth century displaced the members causing the transfer of Ionan power to Dunkeld. Iona is still considered a holy place and although Dunkeld and St Andrews were to supersede it as Scotland's seats of religious power, Iona has never lost its reputation as the country's holy island. It was the place where the MacAlpin kings of Scots were buried, until Donald III Ban, who was buried there in the latter part of the eleventh century. Although in the centuries following Iona lost all its religious influence, Columba did not and his importance as a Scottish saint continued to grow. During the tenth century emblems of Columba were synonymous with victory and later in *Hakon's Saga* King Alexander II's death is attributed to the fact that he attacked Columba's sacred land.

From the reign of William the Lion the image of St Andrew gained force and by the time of Robert the Bruce both saints represented the Church in Scotland. He took the staff of Columba and the emblem of Andrew, the saltire flag, into battle at Bannockburn. However, it was St Andrew who emerged as the country's patron saint.

The magnificent abbey

Inside the abbey

IONA

Iona's ancient spiritual reputation as a place of sanctity and retreat draws pilgrims from all over the world. The island was populated as far back as 5000BC. Mesolithic tools have been excavated near the abbey and archaeologists believe that farming communities were working the land as early as 3500BC. There is evidence of a Bronze Age burial cairn, an Iron Age hill fort and even the Druid worship of the Celtic tribes.

Wild and at the mercy of the elements, perhaps it is not surprising that it suited the monastic lifestyle established by Columba. Its spiritual place in Scotland has been maintained and today Iona is home to an ecumenical Christian community committed to bringing people together and working and praying for justice and peace. Each week from March to October a pilgrimage is arranged around the island from the abbey to the St Oran's chapel. It begins with the ancient stone cross dedicated to St Martin of Tours which is assumed to be one of the markers of St Columba's grave. Standing on the original site it is the only complete cross that survives on Iona although the remains of another four are evident and remnants of these can be found in the abbey museum.

Near the cross are the remains of a bee-hive shaped cell which was uncovered during the 1950s and is believed to be that of St Columba. The cell would have been one of many forming the original settlement along with a small rectangular church, other buildings and farm land.

The abbey church, St Mary's Cathedral, founded by the Lord of the Isles in1203, played an impressive role since the abbot was free from Episcopal jurisdiction.

Rebuilding was carried out in the early fifteenth century when the community was still deriving its revenue from the parishes on neighbouring islands. By the time of the Reformation in 1560, the abbey had gone into decline. In 1874 restoration work was begun by the Duke of Argyll.

Under the direction of the Iona Community work has continued on the buildings including the museum, chapter house and cloisters.

The Abbey (from the sea)

Scotland's Christian heritage and St Columba's holy island are synonymous with each other. Since Columba first landed there more than 1400 years ago, it has remained a place of pilgrimage, a sacred place of prayer and peace.

It is thought that Columba arrived on Iona around 563 with twelve of his fellow monks, as part of his mission to found monasteries and churches in Scotland. It was with the abbey of Iona that his fame was to spread and last throughout the ages. From this monastery he inspired the conversion of Scotland to Christianity. Legend states that when he was an old man he died on the altar of his beloved abbey. Columba was in Iona more than a century after Ninian had established his Candida Casa at Whithorn. We know little of Columba's early life except that he was born to a noble Irish family and lived at a time when Gaels from Ireland were colonising the West of Scotland, intermingling with the Picts and the already Christianised Britons.

Almost everything we know of Columba has come from the writings of Adamnan, ninth abbot of Iona, who recorded stories about the saint and his visions. His work, one of the earliest surviving pieces of literature from Scotland, painted a picture of Columba as a simple and prayerful man and it is this enduring image of him which has lasted throughout the centuries. *'He was angelic in countenance, refined in speech, holy in his works and a man of excellent talents and great counsel.'*

Adamnan's *Vita Sancti Columbae* is not a biography of St Columba but what we have of it provides information on the founding of Scotland's famous holy isle and one of its earliest saints. He explains that Columba and Iona are the Latin and Hebrew words for 'dove', a name he believes was a fitting tribute for his predecessor:

'It is revealed that the Holy Spirit came down in the form of a dove. Similarly in the gospel our Saviour instructed His disciples to have the simplicity of the dove, for the dove is a simple and innocent bird. And so it was right that a simple and innocent man, who by his dove-like character made a dwelling within himself for the Holy Spirit, should be called by his name.'

For thirty-four years Columba lived on the island, spending his days working, reading, writing and praying:

'By day and night he was engaged also in the unwearying labours of fast and vigil. And through all this he was beloved by all for the happiness that always shone in his holy face.'

Adamnan pointed out that:

'Columba was no ordinary man and his greatness and holiness had been foretold before he was born when his mother was greeted by an angel. He possessed the ability to perform miracles, to see visions of angels and remarkable prophetic powers which not only allowed him to see into the future but also to witness contemporary events which were happening many miles away.'

The resemblance with Christ does not end with the angel visiting his mother and the twelve accompanying him to Iona, but also in the miracles which Adamnan attributes to Columba. Adamnan described his first miracle thus:

'Young Columba was visiting St Findbarr, an Irish bishop, when they ran out of wine to celebrate a feast day Mass.

House of prayer Iona

According to Scottish historians, this dispute was inevitable since Iona was by this time out of step with the Church in Ireland and the Northumbrian Church. Tension was to continue throughout the seventh century between the Celtic and Roman Church of England, Ireland and Pictland.

In response the abbots of Iona blasted Wilfred, the Lindisfarne monk who later became Bishop of Ripon, for his attack on Columba. When Adamnan later produced his work the figure of Columba was removed from the world of politics into which Wilfred had dragged him and was concerned only with the saint. As a result Adamnan omits to mention the founding of Lindisfarne in 635 by the Columban church of Iona and instead concentrates solely on Colum Cille as a simple man of God.

Columba then drew water from the well and invoking the name of Jesus, who turned water into wine at the wedding in Cana, turned the well water into wine.

This, then, was the first proof of miraculous power that Christ the Lord made manifest through His disciple, the same that He had wrought through Himself in Cana of Galilee as the beginning of His miraculous signs.'

There is more to Adamnan's work than simply recording the piety of Columba, for it was also an exercise in PR, a very effective one which stopped the cult of Columba being called into question. His work was written some twenty-five years after the Synod of Whitby, where Columba's reputation and the leadership of Iona was challenged by another strand of the Church, that of Northumbria which had sprung up under Aidan on Lindisfarne in the 630s.

FRICTION BETWEEN THE CLERGY

IN OCTOBER 1832 Pope Gregory XVI appointed Andrew Carruthers Vicar-apostolic of the Eastern District. The Church was continuing to expand and extend its influence. In the capital city, adherents had increased from 700 to 8,000 and from 50 to 24,000 in Glasgow. Twenty-two churches had been erected in just a few years.

The Catholic population of the Western District comprised immigrant Irish, driven from their homeland by the 1845-6 famine and seeking work from the industries in the commercial centres of Scotland. The situation led to some friction between the indigenous clergy and the Irish newcomers.

The latter thought themselves slighted in the distribution of ecclesiastical offices. They publicly showed these sentiments through the auspices of the Glasgow Free Press, whose editor supported their case.

The divide widened when the Irish clergy submitted resolutions to Rome stating their grievances. It was a sign of the emerging self-confidence of the Catholic community in Scotland that there were sufficient numbers to subdivide into factions. The opposing party dispatched a report to Bishop Murdoch disputing the accusations of favouritism. The bishop was not implicated in the furore but the fracas contributed to his untimely death in 1865.

His successor, Bishop Gray, received from the Holy See as his coadjutor an Irish Vincentian father named Lynch. The strategy behind this move by Rome was to ensure that the elevation of an Irishman would placate both parties.

In 1867 the Vatican selected the Archbishop of Westminster, Monsignor Manning, to intercede in the dispute and offer viable solutions. His report of the situation stated, 'that there appeared little prospect of a fusion of the two parties'. When the friction between the Scottish and Irish parties in Glasgow reached new heights, the Irish contingent called for the restoration of the Catholic hierarchy.

It was in the pages of the pro-Irish Free Press that this demand was addressed to the Holy See on the basis that the Vicars-apostolic were irredeemably prejudiced against the Irish-born Catholics. Many of the Irish clergy in Glasgow supported the stance and it fell to the Vicars-apostolic of Scotland and their English counterparts to give their views on the matter.

Cardinal Wiseman had written in 1864,

'In my opinion there is no room to doubt that a thorough change is required in the ecclesiastical organisation of Scotland.

'An increase in the number of Vicars-apostolic would naturally appear to be advisable in the first place: at the same time, many difficulties would be overcome were the existing form of Church government to be modified by the nomination of ordinary bishops.'

Bishops Murdoch and Gray of Western District and Bishop Kyle of Northern District expressed the collective opinion that restoration of the hierarchy would not be advantageous and could arouse further prejudice against the progress of Catholicism in Scotland.

In contrast, Archbishop Manning, considered that:

'There seems to me only one means of remedying the existing evils and guarding against them for the future – namely, the erection of dioceses in Scotland and the introduction of a regular hierarchy.'

The preparations for the restoration of the Scottish hierarchy, after several years of apathy, were renewed during the celebration of the episcopal jubilee of Pius IX. A deputation of Scottish Catholics conveyed to the Pontiff greetings of fidelity and Bishop Strain, presented an emotional address:

'Distant Scotland, the Ultima Thule, comes forward with the other nations of the world to offer her homage.

'Once a most faithful handmaid of the Holy See, up to the time of the great apostasy of the sixteenth century, which among us was brought about more by foreign influence than by national causes, she now begins again to put forth blossoms of faith and to produce seemly fruits.

'And when your Holiness shall be pleased to establish among us the ecclesiastical hierarchy, as you have already *done in England, there will be given a fresh impetus to religion and many will return to the faith of their fathers.'*

In reply the Pope expressed his delight at the presence of so many distinguished Scottish Catholics and observed that he was well aware that the country's literary reputation and noble buildings of the capital had gained it the title of the Modern Athens. He added that however much he admired the taste and culture of the nation he cherished more in his heart the conversion of its people.

The restoration of the hierarchy would come in 1878.